THE SUPER BOOK OF
FOOTBALL

J. David Miller

A *Sports Illustrated For Kids* Book

Dedicated to Leesa Anne, who always believed.

My thanks goes out to several friends for their help in this effort, including Kevin Thomas, the best Little League quarterback in America; Michael Smith, who has taught me what courage is all about; the Hixson Wildcats; Mike Haskew, for his outstanding research efforts on this project; the National Football League, for its cooperation; Justin Glanville, a coaching legend in the making; John Butler and the rest of the Buffalo Bills; and Mouse Davis, who will someday get the credit for being the great coach he is. Thanks also to my editor, Richard Amdur, for his patience and hard work on this project.

Design layout by Armen Kojoyian

First Edition

Library of Congress Cataloging-in-Publication Data

Miller, J. David (Joseph David), 1964–
    The super book of football / by J. David Miller. — 1st ed.
       p.   cm.
    "A Sports Illustrated for kids book."
    Summary: Traces the history of football, discusses Superbowl championships, and highlights college and professional record holders.
    ISBN 0-316-57370-1
    1. Football—History—Juvenile literature. [1. Football—History.] I. Title.
GV950.7.M5 1990
796.332′2—dc20
                                     89-29604
                                     CIP
                                     AC

SPORTS ILLUSTRATED FOR KIDS is a trademark of THE TIME INC. MAGAZINE COMPANY.

Sports Illustrated for Kids Books is a joint imprint of Little, Brown and Company and Warner Juvenile Books. This title is published in arrangement with Cloverdale Press Inc.

10 9 8 7 6 5 4 3 2 1

RRD OH

For further information regarding this title, write to Little, Brown and Company, 34 Beacon Street, Boston, MA 02108

Published simultaneously in Canada by Little, Brown & Company (Canada) Limited

Printed in the United States of America

Photography Credits

Walter Ioss, Jr./Sports Illustrated: 16, 46, 80, 81, 88, 89

Neil Leifer/Sports Illustrated: 13, 36, 83, 87, 99

John Iacono/Sports Illustrated: 42, 48, 67, 101

Richard Mackson/Sports Illustrated: 43, 73, 118

Heinz Kluetmeier/Sports Illustrated: 39, 100

Peter Read Miller/Sports Illustrated: 19, 108

Jerry Wachter/Sports Illustrated: 85

James Drake/Sports Illustrated: 20

Ronald C. Modra/Sports Illustrated: 43

John D. Hanlon/Sports Illustrated: 96

Bill Smith/Sports Illustrated: 105

Damian Strohmeyer/Sports Illustrated: 107

Andy Havy/Sports Illustrated: 47

Marvin E. Newman/Sports Illustrated: 28

AP/Wide World Photos: 6, 7, 8, 9, 11, 21, 23, 35, 38, 53, 54, 55, 65, 69, 71, 73, 78, 79, 82, 82, 84, 90, 93, 97, 115, 116, 119

Rick Stewart/All-Sport: 63, 69, 92, 102

Will Hart/All-Sport: 34, 67

Jonathan Daniel/All-Sport: 75

Allen Steel/All-Sport: 111, 113

Tim DeFrisco/All-Sport: 104

Brian Masck/All-Sport: 103

Robert Beck/All-Sport: 109

Stephen Dunn/All-Sport: 125

Scott Halleran/All-Sport: 120

Doug Pensinger/All-Sport: 124

Otto Gruele, Jr./All-Sport: 68

All-Sport: 108

Al Messerschmidt: 15, 17, 26, 27, 29, 33, 49, 61, 65, 66, 70, 76, 103, 117

Fred Roe: 12, 14, 45, 74, 78, 80, 87

Mike Malarkey: 18, 40, 112, 123, 126

Mike Valeri/FPG International: 38, 71, 91

UPI/Bettman Newsphotos: 4, 25

NFL Photos: 58, 60

Rod Hana/NFL Photos: 56

Tony Tomsic/NFL Photos: 59

Malcolm W. Emmons/NFL Photos: 86

Dallas Cowboys: 120

David Madison: 41, 64, 72, 74

CONTENTS

FOREWORD
by
Herschel Walker

I can't talk to you about football without talking about fitness. No one can play football without being physically fit. And I'm concerned about the fact that so many kids in this country aren't in good shape. According to the President's Council on Physical Fitness, approximately 50% of girls ages 6 through 17, and 30% of boys ages 6 through 12 cannot run a mile in less than 10 minutes. That's pretty slow! If you were that slow and were playing football, you'd get tackled the second you touched the ball.

I know that growing up is hard. You have a lot of responsibilities: school, chores around the house, sports programs. Sometimes you feel you've just had enough. You've tried to do everything to the best of your ability, but it seems that nothing turns out well enough to satisfy the grown-ups.

The thing you've got to remember is that you must be honest with yourself. Being honest means that *you* have to feel good about what you're doing, whether it's playing football or studying hard or working out. You can't do it for somebody else. As long as you give everything you try a fair shake, no one can ask for more.

But I want to ask everybody—kids and grown-ups—to put more effort into becoming physically fit and staying that way. Working out is not just something you should do to get in shape to play football or some other sport. You should do it so that you can feel good about yourself and ready to tackle anything. Even the San Francisco 49ers!

AUTHOR'S NOTE

There's something about the game of football that makes it more exciting than any other sport. Maybe that's because it's so packed with power and hard-hitting action. But football today, particularly pro football, is much more than just head-banging. To really appreciate the game, you have to understand it, and that's what this book is all about.

In recent years I have written hundreds of articles and several books on the great sport of football. I've also taught the game to hundreds of boys and watched them mature into young men. But I can honestly say that playing the game myself was one of the biggest thrills of my life. There's nothing like the feeling that buzzes from your head to your toes when you complete a perfect pass or when you're sprinting breathlessly for a 75-yard touchdown! And no other game offers such inspiring examples of sportsmanship, fitness and courage.

The history of football is filled with great men who made many contributions to the game. Each new season presents fresh opportunities for today's players to become tomorrow's champions. Whether you play football yourself or just like watching the game and reading about it, it's my hope that this book will increase your enjoyment of this thrilling, action-packed sport!

—*J. David Miller*

SECTION I:

★ ★ ★ ★ ★

THE ORIGINS OF FOOTBALL

★ ★ ★ ★ ★

CHAPTER 1
IN THE BEGINNING

BLOOD AND GUTS: THE HISTORY OF FOOTBALL

Modern football coaches order players "to use their heads" when playing the game. It seems funny, then, that the game of football began with somebody using a head—literally.

Hundreds of years ago, around 1046, England was conquered by Denmark and occupied by the Danes. The English didn't want the Danish people in their country, and finally forced them to leave after many bloody battles.

A few years later, an English boy was walking through an old battleground. He uncovered a Danish skull left over from England's war with Denmark. Because Denmark was the enemy, the boy began kicking the skull around the field. Soon other boys joined him. But some of them were barefoot, and it hurt to kick the skull. So another boy had the bright idea to replace the skull with an inflated cow bladder. The boys kicked and ran with it until someone tackled them, the way kids do today when they play "kill the man with the ball."

INJURED PLAYERS DIED IN THE STREETS

By the 12th century (about 100 years later), grown men were playing football. There were sometimes 100 players or more from the same town on each team. When the cow bladder was thrown down, the game was on. The team that could run the "ball" into the middle of the rival town was the winner. The players were nasty troublemakers. When they charged into town, yelling and kicking the ball, frightened villagers would run inside and close their doors. There were no rules. Women and children who got in the way were trampled, and any player who wore padding was called a sissy. Instead of wearing helmets, players grew their hair long to protect their skulls. Noses were broken, teeth were knocked out, and arms and legs were fractured. Injured players were often left to die in the streets.

The game became so violent that football players were ordered not to play all over town, but on vacant fields. The players marked off a field with boundaries and established some rules. Though they agreed that both teams should have the same number of players, there were still often as many as 50 players on a team. The game was very popular among soldiers. But when the soldiers started spending more time playing football than practicing their military maneuvers, the king of England banned the sport. Anyone who was caught playing football was sent to jail.

For the next 400 years, the only men who played football in England were criminals. The ban was finally lifted in 1603, and when football became legal again, it was strictly *foot*ball. Passing or running with the ball, even touching it with anything except the feet, was against the rules in an effort to prevent the bloody battles that had given the sport a bad name. A standard-size playing field was developed, and points were scored by kicking the ball across the opposing team's goal line. Today this form of football is called soccer.

While the English were playing their version of the game, the Irish had also taken up football and changed it. They liked the wide field, the run-

ning and the goal-scoring, but they decided to allow players to punch the ball forward with their fists. This made the game more violent again, because many players intentionally missed the ball and punched their opponents instead. Irish football became a cross between boxing and soccer, and dozens of fights broke out in every game. The Irish called their version of the sport Gaelic football.

THE FIRST TOUCHDOWN

It was the English, however, who took the biggest step in the development of modern football. During a soccer game at Rugby College in 1823, a player named William

Ellis was having trouble kicking the ball. To the surprise of his teammates, he picked it up and ran the length of the field, then dove into the goal with the football. It was the first "touchdown" in history. William Ellis got into big trouble, but the fans had screamed wildly when he made his move, so Rugby College decided to change the rules. Players were allowed to run with the ball until they were tackled. This became known as Rugby football.

Although rugby became very popular in England, soccer was still the country's favorite sport. When the English finally brought football to America, it was soccer, not rugby, that was first played there. The first American football (soccer) game was played in 1869, between Rutgers University and Princeton University in New Jersey.

In 1874 the soccer team from Harvard College in Massachusetts challenged McGill University of Montreal, Canada, to come down and play a game of football. McGill accepted the challenge. But when McGill's team arrived, it was a rugby team, not a soccer team! After much arguing, the two teams arrived at a compromise: They would play half the game under rugby rules and the other half under soccer rules. The Harvard players decided that they preferred the tough sport of rugby. They asked Yale, a rival university, to start playing rugby, too. Soon the annual rugby match between Yale and Harvard became a violent clash that attracted thousands of spectators. Thus Yale, Harvard and Princeton dominated the early years of college football in America.

THE FATHER OF AMERICAN FOOTBALL

In 1880 a man named Walter Camp made basic changes in rugby that brought the game a step closer to modern football. Camp invented the scrimmage line, where only one team at a time had possession of the ball. (In rugby, the two teams struggle over possession of the ball in a kind of huddle called a scrum.) The ball was put in play when it was "snapped" or tossed backward between the legs to a player acting as quarterback, which would one day become the most glamorous position in the game. Because of this, Walter Camp is often called the father of American football.

In the early days the scoring system favored field goals (kicks over the goalpost) *over* touchdowns (running or throwing the ball over the goal line). As late as 1884, a safety (when the offensive team is tackled in its own end zone) was worth one point, a touchdown was worth two, the "point" after the touchdown was worth four, and a field goal five. By the early 1890's, touchdowns were worth five points, the same as field goals, but extra points dropped down to one and a safety became two.

New rules in 1888 brought another radical change to the game. Up to this time tackling was allowed only from the waist up, which was a common rule in rugby. But in 1888 players decided to allow tackling as low as the knees. Furthermore, linemen or blockers were ordered to keep their arms at their sides instead of extending their arms. It was popular at that time to surround the ball carrier tightly with blockers, making it nearly impossible to tackle the man with the ball.

The Famous "Turgleback" Formation

In 1890 Amos Alonzo Stagg, who had been a famous player at Yale, began coaching college football at the University of Chicago. He was credited with inventing several formations, including the "turgleback" formation, where a team gathered into an oval formation and drove at the defense. Eventually the turgleback formation straightened out and became something called a T formation, in which the center and the quarterback form the trunk of the T and the backs line up behind them parallel to the line of scrimmage and form the top of the T. This became the standard formation of football.

Football strategy progressed as more and more colleges took up the game. Though rules differed in almost every league, one thing stayed the same: The game was violent in any form. Harvard invented a formation known as the "flying wedge." Huge linemen with suitcase handles sewed onto the backs of their shirts would thunder downfield, holding onto one another's handles, while the ball carrier ran behind them. The flying wedge led to many injuries.

While colleges made football popular, the game was also being played between local athletic clubs. One result of the fierce rivalries that developed between several Pittsburgh-area clubs was the first professional football player. William "Pudge" Heffelfinger, who had been a star player at Yale, was paid $500 by the Allegheny Athletic Association to play against the Pittsburgh Athletic Association in 1892. The AAA won when Heffelfinger returned a fumble 35 yards for a touchdown. In the following years contracts between players and athletic clubs were common. Sometimes players would play for their college one day, then play for the athletic club the next.

In 1899 a man named Chris O'Brien formed a neighborhood team in Chicago called the Morgan Athletic Club. The club changed its name later to the Chicago Cardinals, which then became the St. Louis Cardinals, and most recently the Phoenix Cardinals of the National Football League. The Cardinals are football's oldest professional team. In 1900 a man named William C. Temple began paying all the players for the Duquesne Country and Athletic Club, making him the first known "owner" of a football team.

How Did a Baseball Team Win a Football Game?

Baseball actually helped professional football get started. The players on the Philadelphia Athletics baseball team and the Philadelphia Phillies players formed professional football teams. They joined the Pittsburgh Stars and several other teams, and named the new league the National Football League. In the first game ever played in the new league, the Athletics won, 39–0, over Kanaweola on November 21, 1902.

Many years before the Super Bowl became the championship of pro football, the NFL held a "World Series of Football," just like baseball. It was a five-team tournament. Only about 3,000 people watched the title game. Syracuse won the first football World Series in 1902. In 1903 the Franklin Athletic Club won the second and last World Series of pro football.

Violence in college and pro football continued on into the 1900s. In 1905 18 people died and 159 were critically injured playing football. One key injury happened to a huge lineman named Bob Maxwell, who played for Swarthmore College. In a game against the University of Pennsylvania, Maxwell was attacked on every play. After the game he had to be helped from the field because he had been so badly hurt. President Theodore Roosevelt saw a picture of the injured Maxwell in a newspaper and became angry at the violence of the sport. He threatened to ban football unless it became safer.

The year 1905 was also known for the "Heston massacre," which involved the great running back from the University of Michigan, Billy Heston. When Heston left Michigan, three teams bid for his services. Heston was arrogant and asked for $1,000, which today would be like asking for $1 million. All three teams refused to pay him, so he missed an entire season. The next season Heston finally signed with Canton for $600. In his first pro game against Massillon, he didn't gain an inch though he hammered at the Massillon defense all game long. In his next game, against Chicago, Heston's leg was broken badly; the injury ended his professional career and became known as the "Heston massacre."

In an effort to open up the game, the forward pass was legalized and the flying wedge was made illegal in 1906. But nobody threw the football until 1913, when two Notre Dame players named Gus Dorais and Knute Rockne used the pass for the first time in a sensational victory over West Point. Until the mid-1930s, the forward pass was considered extremely dangerous, and was only used when the game was nearly over and a team was desperate for victory. The first completed pass in a professional game occurred when George Parratt of the Massillon Tigers threw a touchdown to Dan "The Bullet" Riley.

While a few long—and successful—touchdown passes forced defenses to change their way of thinking, a great Native American running back

Jim Thorpe, pictured here in 1912, the year he also won the Olympic decathlon

was exciting fans and teammates with his fierce running style. His name was Jim Thorpe, a double gold-medal winner at the 1912 Olympics and a football and track star for the Carlisle Indian School in Pennsylvania. Thorpe, who signed with the Canton Bulldogs for $250 a game, led his team to three consecutive championships in the Ohio League.

WHY WOULD YOU NAME A TEAM THE PACKERS?

During the early 1900s pro football was played mostly in the Northeast—states like Ohio, Illinois and Pennsylvania. In 1919 Earl "Curly" Lambeau and

George Calhoun started a team in Green Bay, Wisconsin. The Indian Packing Company agreed to pay $500 for equipment and supplies. The team called itself the Packers after the name of its sponsor, and practiced on a company field.

But by 1920 nearly all pro football teams were suffering from the same problems. First of all, every team had different rules, and dozens of "leagues" existed. Players were moving from team to team depending on who would pay the most. One account reveals that the great Knute Rockne played for *six* teams in one season. Can you imagine Eric Dickerson or Dan Marino changing teams every week, jumping to the team that offered them more money?

Another problem was that some teams would use college stars who were still in school. That would be like watching a running back for Notre Dame run for two touchdowns on Saturday for the Fighting Irish, then play the next day for the Indianapolis Colts.

So the owners of most professional teams decided that, to be fair, there should be a single league with the same rules for everybody. The league was called the American Professional Football Association. A franchise cost only $100. But the league had little money, and throughout its first season in 1920, it was very disorganized and hardly had any rules. The owners met again in 1921 and increased the league to 22 teams. A constitution, or list of rules, was then established. And a playoff system was developed so that the league would have a champion at season's end. Chicago's Staleys, under the direction of player-coach George Halas, won the first league title with a 9–1–1 record.

A year later, in 1922, the league changed its name to the National Football League and reorganized again, this time fielding 18 teams. The Chicago Staleys changed their name, too, and they became the Chicago Bears. In a game in 1923 George Halas, who was still playing *and* coaching the Bears, picked up a Jim Thorpe fumble and ran 98 yards for a touchdown, setting a record for longest touchdown run that would last until 1972.

THE BARNSTORMING BEARS

George Halas's T formation offense was unstoppable behind quarterback Sid Luckman. Halas was the first coach to tell his center not to *look* through his legs at the quarterback when snapping the ball but to keep his head up. Back then, all centers were poor blockers because they looked through their legs. Halas developed more plays than any other coach and many other pro and college teams copied his success.

Soon teams were using pass receivers and an occasional man-in-motion (when pass receivers move before the ball is snapped to start a play),

Red Grange, star running back for the Chicago Bears, shown here in 1923 while playing for the University of Illinois

Running back Ernie Nevers

which loosened up the game. Passers were throwing the ball with deadly accuracy, but running backs were still the biggest attraction of the young NFL. In 1925 Harold "Red" Grange, an All-American halfback from Illinois, signed a contract to play with Halas's Chicago Bears. Grange was an NFL sensation—a Thanksgiving crowd of 36,000, at that time the largest in history, turned out to see Grange and the Bears play the Chicago Cardinals to a scoreless tie.

The Bears were the NFL's most popular team. They set out on a "barnstorming" tour, playing 8 games in 12 days in the cities. Fans turned out by the thousands to see Grange. A crowd of 73,000 watched the Bears play the New York Giants, and in Los Angeles, 75,000 watched the Bears whip the Los Angeles Tigers.

WHAT IF JOHN ELWAY OWNED HIS OWN TEAM?

In 1926 Red Grange decided he wouldn't play for the Bears anymore unless they tripled his salary. The Bears told him to take a hike. So Grange started his own league, the American Football League, and his own team, the New York Yankees. That would be like John Elway getting angry at the Denver Broncos and going off to start his own league! But Grange's new league ran out of money and folded after one year.

That same year George Halas of the Bears developed a rule that made it illegal for a pro team to sign a player whose class had not graduated from college. That rule, though modified, is still enforced today.

By this time the NFL had grown to 22 teams. The Duluth Eskimos signed Stanford University's All-American fullback Ernie Nevers, whose popularity was equal to that of Red Grange. The Eskimos once played 29 games in a single season, including 28 road games, and Nevers played every game. At the end of the year Nevers had only missed 29 *minutes* in 29 games. In those days you were teased if you *didn't* play an entire game. Players either played 60 minutes or were carried off on a stretcher. There weren't separate teams for offense and defense. The best players "went both ways," as it's called.

Native American Jim Thorpe continued to dominate the early years of the NFL. Thorpe seldom ran over his opponents, but avoided tackles by twisting his hips in a way that would make tacklers miss him. Thorpe also fastened a piece of sheet metal to his shoulder pads. When someone tried to tackle him—*bam!*—the metal would knock them silly. He wore the metal shoulder pads until 1925, his final year in football with the New York Giants. To this day, people still argue that Thorpe might have been the greatest running back in the history of the NFL. If Thorpe were coming out of college today, he would be a first-round draft pick and would probably make more than $1 million a year.

Ernie Nevers continued his assault on the NFL well into 1929. In one game that year he alone scored six rushing touchdowns and four extra points to beat Red Grange and the Chicago Bears, 40–6. Nevers' 40 points in a game by a single player is a record that still stands today.

During the early days of pro football many fans believed that good college teams were better than professional teams. The NFL lacked credibility. So in 1930 the Giants agreed to play a team of former Notre Dame players coached by Knute Rockne. A crowd of 55,000 gathered at the stadium, the first truly big crowd to see a professional football game. The Giants won easily, prompting thousands of fans to put their stamp of approval on the NFL. But they still clamored for a faster, more exciting game.

In 1933, the NFL obliged them. Since its inception, the NFL had followed the rules of college football. But now it made significant changes to create a more thrilling game and increase fan support. The NFL introduced hash marks and goalposts and split the league into two divisions, with the winner of each division meeting each year in a championship game. The NFL also added several more teams. Believe it or not, many of the new teams had baseball names, such as the Pittsburgh Pirates and the Cincinnati Reds.

What Ever Happened to Jay Berwanger?

The first NFL draft was held on February 8, 1936. The Philadelphia Eagles made University of Chicago halfback and Heisman Trophy winner Jay Berwanger

Running back Jay Berwanger

the first player ever drafted by the NFL. But the money a player could make in football was often less than what he could make at a steady job, so Berwanger turned down the Eagles and the NFL. The first draft pick in history never played a down in the NFL. Alabama's Riley Smith, who was chosen second by Boston, became the first drafted player to sign with the NFL.

Meanwhile at a tiny school called Texas Christian University, a young quarterback named Sammy Baugh was beginning his career. Over the next decade Baugh was to make the most revolutionary change in football to date. He became the most sensational passer in history, chilling his opponents by throwing perfect spirals to speedy receivers. Baugh made the forward pass a routine offensive play. His derring-do resulted in further rule changes and strategy developments that would lead pro football into the modern passing era.

Baugh brought his wide-open passing ways to the NFL when he signed with the Washington Redskins in 1937. All season he frustrated opponents who could not stop his aerial attack, and then led his team to a 28–21 victory over the Bears in the NFL title game. But during the season several teams had taken cheap shots at Baugh in an effort to hurt him. They would hit him long after he threw the ball and knock him down from behind. So the NFL added a rule that made "roughing the passer" illegal. You weren't allowed to hurt the quarterback on purpose or hit him after he threw the ball.

The first Pro Bowl game was held in 1939, but it was a little different from today's Pro Bowl. The league champions played a team of NFL all-stars, which in the opinion of many people made the original version of the Pro Bowl more interesting. Today the Pro Bowl consists of two terms of all-stars chosen by the players.

The NFL at War

Between the years 1942 and 1945 World War II drained the NFL of its players. A total of 638 players joined the armed forces to fight for their country. The Bears George Halas was among them. The NFL continued to play with "replacement" players, most of whom would not have been good enough to play if the regular players had been there. Several teams quit playing until their players came back, but the league rolled on.

Many players who went to war were surprised when they came home. While they were gone the NFL had made several rule changes. The league ordered every player to wear a leather helmet (all this time the players had not been wearing anything on their heads). And the hash marks were moved closer to the center of the field, 20 yards from each sideline. This gave the offense more room to maneuver since it would no longer be "hemmed in" by the near sideline.

Even with so many men in the military, another league started in 1945 to compete with the NFL. It was called the All-America Football Conference, and it began play in 1946, the year after the Japanese surrendered, ending World War II. America's soldiers and most of the NFL's players returned home, though 21 NFL players were killed in the war.

The All-America Football Conference began with eight teams, including the Cleveland Browns, coached by Paul Brown. The Browns would win the title in all four years of the AAFC's existence. In 1950 three teams from the AAFC—the Cleveland Browns, San Francisco 49ers and Baltimore Colts—were merged into the NFL. The rest of the AAFC folded. Most NFL players thought the AAFC was a "sissy" league. The Browns proved them wrong; in their first NFL season Cleveland won the NFL title. In the next 10 years the Brown would play in all 10 NFL championship games!

The NFL took its three new teams and redesigned the league into two conferences. It created a National Conference and an American Conference. By now the NFL was truly a "national" league, with teams from New York to Los Angeles. The Los Angeles Rams were the first team to have all of its games televised, but several other teams began making deals to get their games on TV.

The modern NFL was on its way.

"Slinging" Sammy Baugh in action against the Washington Redskins in 1942

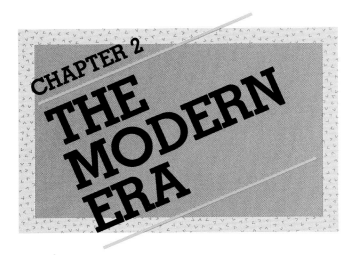

CHAPTER 2
THE MODERN ERA

THE TURNING POINT

December 28, 1958. Snow was falling at Yankee Stadium. After four quarters the New York Giants and Baltimore Colts had played to a 17–17 tie in the NFL Championship. It was the first overtime game in pro football history. Thousands of people were in the stadium, and at least a million more were watching on television. The Colts marched steadily downfield behind the deadly passing of quarterback Johnny Unitas. With the ball on the one-yard line, fullback Alan Ameche crashed through the line for the winning touchdown.

Many people believe that game was the turning point for professional football. The sport became more popular than ever. Every team had its own star player—the Cleveland Browns had Jim Brown and the Green Bay Packers had Bart Starr. The NFL was so exciting that Bert Bell, the league commissioner, died of a heart attack during the last two minutes of a game between the Pittsburgh Steelers and the Philadelphia Eagles in 1959. He was replaced by a man named Pete Rozelle, who was general manager of the Los Angeles Rams.

The demand for football was so great that another league began playing in 1960. The American Football League was organized by Lamar Hunt, a wealthy businessman from Dallas, Texas. The league consisted of the Oakland Raiders, Miami Dolphins, Houston Oilers, Buffalo Bills, Boston Patriots, Kansas City Chiefs and Dallas Cowboys, among others.

The rivalry between the NFL and AFL was fierce. Teams would "hide" players to keep them from signing with the other league. Salaries rose at a fast pace, especially when an Alabama quarterback from the University of Alabama named Joe Namath signed with the New York Jets for $400,000. In 1966 the two leagues spent more than $7 million to sign their draft choices. The NFL signed 75% of the 232 players it drafted, while the AFL signed 46% of the 181 players it drafted.

Later that year the two leagues realized it was getting too expensive to compete for players and fans. American Football League organizer Lamar Hunt, who owned the Kansas City Chiefs and Tex Schramm, the president and general manager of the Dallas Cowboys worked out an agreement. On June 8 Pete Rozelle announced that the two leagues would combine to form an expanded league with 24 teams, to be increased to 26 teams in 1968 and to 28 in the next few years. Both leagues would play separate schedules through 1969. But an AFL-NFL World Championship would be held in January of 1967.

Green Bay Packer quarterback Bart Starr

THE FIRST SUPER BOWL

The Green Bay Packers and the Kansas City Chiefs were the first two teams to play in the championship, which owners called the Super Bowl. It was also the first time an AFL team had played an NFL team. The Green Bay players looked down on the upstart AFL team and called the Chiefs players bad names. Some even said that the AFL was a "Mickey Mouse" operation. The Chiefs were able to keep their sense of humor and when they took the field for Super Bowl I, all the Kansas City players wore Mickey Mouse hats.

At halftime the score was 13–10 in favor of Green Bay, but it had been a close game. In the second half, behind tough coach Vince Lombardi and quarterback Bart Starr, the Packers rolled to a 35–10 victory. The Packers earned $15,000 each for winning, while the Chiefs made $7,500 for losing. The game was held at the Los Angeles Memorial Coliseum in front of a crowd of 61,496 fans. There were 40,000 empty seats. Can you imagine a Super Bowl for which 40,000 people don't show up?

By contrast Super Bowl II was a sellout. It was held in Miami and the NFL made a record $3 million from ticket sales. The Green Bay Packers won again, this time beating the Oakland Raiders. From then on, the Super Bowl would be one of the biggest single-day events in modern sports, attracting enormous television audiences year after year.

A LITTLE GIRL NAMED HEIDI

There was one minute and five seconds remaining in a critical AFL regular-season game between the New York Jets and the Oakland Raiders on November 17, 1968. The Jets were leading 32–30. Across the nation football fans were glued to their television sets. Suddenly the game disappeared. Instead of watching Joe Namath, viewers were seeing *Heidi,* a movie about a little Swiss girl. The game had run a little long and the network had cut away from it to show the movie on time! Not only that, but also the Raiders scored two touchdowns in the last 42 seconds to win the game, 43–32! Thousands of people called NBC to complain. Today no network will leave a game until it is completely over.

But the Jets got revenge. They beat the Raiders, 27–23, in the AFL championship game held six weeks later. With Joe Namath at quarterback, the Jets became the first AFL team to win the Super Bowl, defeating the Baltimore Colts 16–7.

In 1970 the two leagues officially merged, as they had planned. The Baltimore Colts, Cleveland Browns and Pittsburgh Steelers each agreed

Green Bay
Packer coach
Vince Lombardi

an equal share of the television money. Then, in 1982, Rozelle arranged a contract worth more than $2 *billion* for TV rights. Today each NFL team makes more than $15 million a season *before* they sell a single ticket!

One result of this wealth was new and bigger stadiums that allowed more fans to enjoy their favorite sport. Some stadiums even had roofs, like the Superdome in New Orleans, the Astrodome in Houston, the Kingdome in Seattle and the Silverdome in Pontiac, Michigan. The NFL also made numerous rule changes to make passing a more prominent part of the game. By 1981 football had become the most popular sport in America. A *New York Times* newspaper poll revealed that 48% of sports fans liked football compared to 31% for baseball.

to join with the AFL teams to form the American Football Conference. The other NFL teams formed the National Football Conference. Together, both conferences made up the NFL.

That same year the ABC television network purchased the right to broadcast 13 regular-season games that would be played on Monday nights. That was the beginning of Monday Night Football.

The Million-Dollar League

Once the merger was completed the NFL grew into a multimillion-dollar organization. Teams that had cost only $100 to buy in 1920 were suddenly worth an average of $2 million. By 1980 each club would be worth more than $40 million. This was largely due to television. The three major networks—NBC, CBS and ABC—were paying a lot of money for the right to broadcast NFL games each year, and this made the owners rich.

The NFL sold the rights to its championship game in 1951 for $75,000. In 1961 commissioner Pete Rozelle, who was in charge of the NFL, negotiated a season-long contract with NBC, CBS and ABC that was worth $4.6 million. Each team got

If Pee Wee Is Worth Millions, So Are Players

The players knew the owners were making lots of money, and they got mad because they felt they were not being paid in a fair manner. Some people thought that football players already made too much money. But the players pointed out that they were entertainers, just like singers or actors. Madonna made $50 million in a single year. Pee Wee Herman made $22 million in a single year. So, the players asked, why don't famous football players make the same kind of money? "We are entertainers too," said Miami Dolphins quarterback Dan Marino. "Fans watch the game for the players, not the owners."

In 1982 the players told the owners that unless they received a percentage of the profits every year, they were not going to play. The owners thought they were kidding, but the players went on strike, and refused to play. For 57 days there was no pro football in the United States. The players came back after the owners agreed to improve benefits for players. But the owners still refused to give them a percentage of the profits.

The United States Football League was started in 1983 in an effort to get in on the success—and the profits—of the NFL. The USFL played its games in the spring, to avoid direct competition with the NFL. But it was not easy to convince football fans to watch their sport during baseball season. While the USFL was having a hard time attracting viewers, more and more fans were watching games during ''regular'' football season.

In January 1985 for example, the San Francisco 49ers defeated the Miami Dolphins, 38–16, in Super Bowl XIX at Stanford Stadium in Palo Alto, California. The game was viewed on television by more people than any other live event *in history.*

The USFL did not lack for star attractions like Herschel Walker, Kelvin Bryant, Bobby Hebert and Anthony Carter. And wealthy owners like Donald Trump began buying good players away from the NFL. From 1983 through 1985 the USFL signed the Heisman Trophy winner. In 1983 it was University of Georgia tailback Herschel Walker who joined the USFL. In 1984 it was tailback Mike Rozier of the University of Nebraska. And in 1985 quarterback Doug Flutie of Boston College signed up. For the great college players, the USFL paid enormous salaries. Bingham Young University quarterback Steve Young, for instance, was offered a $2.5 million bonus and a $34.5 million contract to sign with the USFL's Los Angeles Express.

As had happened before, when the NFL was struggling with the AFL, salaries and expenses began to rise in the NFL because of competition with the USFL. NFL players would threaten to ''jump'' to the USFL, and the owners of their teams would pay them more money to stay. L.A. Raiders quarterback Marc Wilson, for instance, received a $1 million contract when he threatened to play for Donald Trump's USFL team in New Jersey. But the USFL folded after just three seasons when most of the team owners ran out of money. It was a costly fight for both leagues. USFL owners had spend more than $200 million competing with the NFL. NFL owners had spent more than $100 million competing with the USFL. But the USFL did accomplish something for NFL players: It increased salaries by more than 100% during its three years of operation. It also increased competition in the NFL, since about 250 of the USFL's 500 players were scooped up by NFL teams upon the USFL's demise.

Joe Montana of the San Francisco 49ers—the quarterback and the team of the 1980s

15

The NFL continued to be a successful business and profitable to team owners. By 1985 it was one of the largest money-making enterprises in history. The NFL had grown from a tiny football operation to a huge corporation in less than 60 years!

"THE REFRIGERATOR"

During the 1985 season a Chicago Bear ate his way onto the professional football scene. William "Refrigerator" Perry, a rookie from Clemson University, became famous overnight. The monstrous defensive tackle weighed 350 pounds and buried ball carriers. Then Chicago head coach Mike Ditka put "The Fridge" into a Monday night game against the Green Bay Packers at running back. With the Bears facing third and goal from the Green Bay one-yard line, Perry smashed through the line of scrimmage, knocking defensive players in every direction as he scored the touchdown! A star was born.

The Bears also had zany quarterback Jim McMahon. McMahon wore earrings, shaved his head, and wore messages on the headbands he wore during games. The fans loved him, though many coaches and NFL officials thought he was a little too controversial.

Behind Ditka, the Fridge and the colorful McMahon, the Chicago Bears once again became one of America's most popular teams. And when the Bears beat the New England Patriots in the Super Bowl on January 26, 1986, the game became the most-watched television program in American history with 127 million viewers and another 10 million who listened to the game on radio. The game was also televised in 59 foreign countries; an estimated 300 million Chinese watched a delayed broadcast of the game.

"UPON FURTHER REVIEW..."

In 1986 the NFL agreed to the use of instant replays to help the officials. Coaches, players and fans were complaining that the referees weren't good enough, so the NFL decided to let referees look at television monitors to make sure the calls were good. That season the

William "Refrigerator" Perry blasting through two offensive linemen

Referees trying to make a decision routinely consult another expert—the videotape camera!

FOR PETE'S SAKE

In 1989 Pete Rozelle resigned as commissioner of the NFL after defeating two rival leagues and surviving many lawsuits. Paul Tagliabue, who had worked with the NFL for many years as a lawyer, became the new commissioner. He is credited with bringing fortune and fame to the NFL in his 29 years as commissioner.

Today professional football is a thriving business. Never has the sport been more popular. The 28 teams are still divided into the National and American conferences and then into three regional divisions. The current alignment is as follows:

National Football Conference

Eastern Division — Dallas Cowboys
Philadelphia Eagles
Phoenix Cardinals
Washington Redskins
New York Giants

Central Division — Detroit Lions
Chicago Bears
Green Bay Packers
Minnesota Vikings
Tampa Bay Buccaneers

Western Division — Atlanta Falcons
Los Angeles Rams
New Orleans Saints
San Francisco 49ers

American Football Conference

Eastern Division — Buffalo Bills
Indianapolis Colts
Miami Dolphins
New England Patriots
New York Jets

Central Division — Houston Oilers
Cincinnati Bengals
Cleveland Browns
Pittsburgh Steelers

officials looked at 374 plays and changed the call 38 times. In the playoffs 18 plays were "reviewed" on replay, and 3 were changed. Whenever the officials used replay, the referee would turn on his microphone and either tell the crowd, "upon further review, the play stands as called," or he would announce that the call had been changed.

By 1987 the players were upset again about the financial side of the game although they were making more money than they had been when they went on strike in 1982. They wanted to be able to offer their services to the highest bidder as "free agents." As it was, when a player's contract with a team ran out, he still *belonged* to that team. Baseball players become free agents in 1976 and football players wanted this, too. So the players decided to go on strike again.

This time, though, the owners were ready for them. They had "replacement" players ready. When the regular players walked out, the NFL teams replaced them with former college and USFL players. Fans and the media called the new Buffalo Bills the "Counterfeit" Bills. The Los Angeles Raiders were called the "Traitors." The Philadelphia Eagles were called the "Beagles." But so many fans watched the replacement games that it scared the players and they went back to work after just three weeks. Today, though, the players are still trying to become free agents.

Western Division—Denver Broncos
Kansas City Chiefs
Los Angeles Raiders
San Diego Chargers
Seattle Seahawks

Pro football, like other professional sports, has some problems. Owners and players file lawsuits. Some players have gotten into trouble by taking drugs or breaking other laws. But this isn't true of every player or team. The NFL has many great players and millions of fans. As you will learn in this book, the NFL is full of funny stories, great players and coaches. Football is very much like life—you only get out of it what you put into it.

Beasts of the East! New York Giants running back Joe Morris looking for some running room.

Variations of the Game

Professional football is not only played in the National Football League. Another form of pro football began in 1986 and is known to American fans as *Arena Football*. The field is half the size of an NFL field, and each team fields just 8 players, instead of 11. The game is played in hockey and basketball arenas, and padded walls surround the playing area. The players are often great college athletes who are just a little too small for the NFL.

The important thing in "Arenaball," as it's affectionately called, is endurance. Players are required to play both offense and defense, which puts a premium on conditioning. The game has proved to be very violent, but it is quite popular among fans.

In Canada the Canadian Football League plays yet another form of the game. The field is much *larger* than an NFL field, and the CFL plays with different rules.

Canadian football teams are allowed to have 12 players on the field instead of 11, and they are allowed only three downs instead of four. The end zones are 25 yards deep, as opposed to 10 yards in the NFL. The Canadian field is 110 yards long and 65 yards wide while an NFL field is 100 yards long and just 53 yards wide.

Canadian football, much like its American cousin, has a rich history. As you may recall, on May 15, 1874, students from Montreal's McGill University crossed the border to play a game of soccer with Harvard University. From this game the Canadian Rugby Union was formed, and it became the sport's first governing body. In 1907 a league was formed, and Canada's governor, Earl Grey, donated a championship cup to the league in 1909. Today Canada's Super Bowl is still known as the Grey Cup game, in honor of Earl Grey.

As rugby gradually evolved into football in America, so it did in Canada. By 1921 Canadian football was very much like the American version. But over the years it changed. In 1958 the Canadian Football League was born. Today there are eight teams in the CFL, and football is one of that country's top spectator sports. The Canadian season begins the first weekend in July and runs through the end of November.

Roughly half of each Canadian team is made up of American football players who didn't make it in the NFL. But occasionally, the CFL contributes to the NFL. Joe Theismann, a long-time great with the Washington Redskins, played several years for the Toronto Argonauts. Warren Moon, who now quarterbacks the Houston Oilers, led the Edmonton Eskimos to five Grey Cup championships.

FOOTBALL AROUND THE WORLD

The popularity of the NFL has attracted football fans around the globe, especially in England, where hundreds of amateur teams have started playing American tackle football. (They have been able to watch NFL games once a week for years now, and the Super Bowl is very big in Great Britain.) In 1991 a new league, called the World League of American Football, will bring Europe a professional league for the first time. The WLAF consists of 10 teams in England, Finland, France, Germany, Italy, the Netherlands, Spain and Sweden as well as several teams in the United States. The WLAF plays by American rules, and looks like a junior NFL. The season begins each year in April and ends with a championship game in July.

COLLEGE FOOTBALL

The National Collegiate Athletic Association (NCAA) is the governing body of college football, setting rules and standards. Many NFL stars come from the college ranks by way of a draft, where they are chosen one at a time by the pro teams. Although the rules prohibit college stars from being paid as

pro players are, many talented players are offered football scholarships, which pay all or part of the bill for their college education.

College football's many different conferences feature many different styles of play. In the Big 10 Conference, the preferred style of attack is usually a slug-mouth, grind-it-out running game. In the Southeastern Conference, teams throw as often as they run.

Part of the excitement of college football comes from the number of fans that attend the games.

Pests of the West! Lineman Howie Long of the Raiders. The Raiders have a bad-boy reputation on and off the field.

Tony Dorsett of the Dallas Cowboys, 1976 winner of the Heisman Trophy as that year's top college player, receives some sideline advice.

People in each state support the major universities, and the games attract huge crowds. The University of Tennessee and the University of Michigan both average more than 100,000 fans every time their teams play. More than three times as many people watch college football games as NFL games. Bob Zuppke, a former college coach, once said that "professional football is motion, college football is emotion."

College football is also big business. The best college coaches make as much as, and sometimes more than NFL head coaches. Virtually every NFL head coach learned his trade as a college coach.

Much like the Pittsburgh Steelers of the 1970s and the San Francisco 49ers of the 1980s, there have been several "teams of the decade" in college football. Michigan, for instance, went undefeated for 56 games between 1901 and 1905. In 1901 they went 11–0, scored 550 points (an average of 55 a game) and held all 11 of their opponents *scoreless.*

New ideas and better athletes over the years have changed the way the professional game is played, and college football has changed as well. College football teams use many more experimental formations than pro teams, often trying ideas that are considered unsound. Professional teams are stocked with talented players, while college teams often must center their attacks around just two or three stars.

The best college teams square off each year in annual bowl games, and the winners of these games are considered the top 10 or 12 teams in the country. College football has no playoff system like the NFL, although college officials are hoping to have a playoff system soon for bowl-game winners to determine a true national champion. Under the current system the media picks a national champion from among the top two or three teams in the country.

College football is critical to professional football because it serves as a minor league where young players can master their skills. Every year the NFL holds a draft, when its 28 teams divide up the best college players in the country. The lowest ranking teams choose first, which gives them the best chance of improving over the coming years.

PRO FOOTBALL HISTORY TIME LINE

1896—The Allegheny Athletic Association fielded the first completely professional team for its abbreviated two-game season.

1897—The Latrobe Athletic Association football team went entirely professional, becoming the first team to play a full season with only professionals.

1904—Halfback Charles Follis signed a contract with the Shelby Athletic Club, making him the first known black football player.

1922—The NFL fielded 18 teams, including the Oorang Indians. The Indians consisted of Native Americans, including such stars as Jim Thorpe, Joe Guyon and Pete Calac. The Indians were sponsored by the Oorang dog kennel.

1932—An NFL playoff game was held indoors for the first time in history. Because of bitter cold and heavy snow in Chicago, the Bears played the Portsmouth Spartans in Chicago Stadium, a basketball arena with only an 80-yard "field." Goal posts were moved from the end lines to the goal lines. The Bears won 9–0.

1934—Beattie Feathers, a rookie running back with the Chicago Bears, became the NFL's first 1,000-yard rusher. He gained 1,004 yards on 101 carries.

1934—The Thanksgiving Day game between the Bears and the Detroit Lions became the first NFL game broadcast nationally on radio. The announcer was Graham McNamee for CBS.

December 9, 1934—The NFL championship game between the Bears and the New York Giants was played under extremely cold and icy conditions. At halftime, players for the Giants removed their cleats and put on basketball sneakers to improve traction on the ice. It worked. That game became known as the "Sneakers Game."

1938—Rookie running back Byron "Whizzer" White of the Pittsburgh Pirates led the NFL in rushing. He later became a Supreme Court Justice.

1938—NBC broadcast a football game between the Brooklyn Dodgers and the Philadelphia Eagles, making it the first NFL game ever televised. Approximately 1,000 people watched the game on television.

January 15, 1939—The New York Giants defeated the NFL All-Stars, 13–10, in the first Pro Bowl.

March 1, 1941—Elmer Layden was named the first commissioner of the NFL. On April 5, NFL headquarters was moved to Chicago.

April 7, 1943—The NFL adopted free substitution rules. This allowed coaches to take a player out

George Halas (left) and Red Grange at ceremonies marking the retirement of three jersey numbers worn by Chicago Bears. Number 56 was worn by receiver Bill Hewitt and number 3 by fullback Bronko Nagurski. Grange is shown here wearing his own number 77 for the last time.

of the game, at any position or at any time, for any reason.

April 21, 1944—The Chicago Cardinals and Pittsburgh Steelers were granted permission to merge for one year under the name Card-Pitt. The merger came about due to lack of funds. It dissolved on the last day of the season, December 3.

January 11, 1946—Bert Bell, the co-owner of the Steelers, became the new NFL commissioner. He moved the NFL's headquarters from Chicago to Philadelphia.

December 15, 1946—Commissioner Bert Bell questioned running backs Frank Filchock and Merle Hapes of the New York Giants about gambling. A gambler had attempted to pay Filchock and Hapes to "fix" the Giants championship game with the Bears, meaning they would play poorly on purpose in order to lose the game. Bell suspended Hapes but allowed Filchock to play. The Bears won 24–14.

January 14, 1948—Plastic helmets were outlawed in the NFL. At the same time, officials approved a plastic tee for kickoffs.

1948—Los Angeles halfback Frank Gehrke painted horns on the Rams helmets. It was the first helmet emblem in professional football.

1949—The NFL had two 1,000-yard rushers in the same season for the first time, Steve Van Buren of Philadelphia and Tony Canadeo of Green Bay.

January 18, 1951—The NFL ruled that tackles, guards and centers were not eligible to catch a forward pass.

1952—The Pittsburgh Steelers were the last professional team to abandon the single-wing offense for the T formation.

1955—The National Football League Players Association was founded. The union stated that its purpose would be to "uphold the rights of the American professional football player."

1955—The Baltimore Colts made an 80¢ phone call to a free agent quarterback named Johnny Unitas. Unitas, who had been cut by the Steelers, signed with the Colts and later became one of the greatest quarterbacks in the history of the game.

1956—The popular techniques of slamming down an opponent by his facemask became illegal. The "facemask tackle" was the most brutal form of tackling. Before the rule change, "facemasking" was only legal when used against a ballcarrier.

1956—CBS became the first television network to broadcast regular-season games.

1958—Jim Brown of the Cleveland Browns gained 1,527 yards rushing in a single season, an NFL record.

1959—An assistant coach named Vince Lombardi was named head coach of the Green Bay Packers. Lombardi would go on to create one of the greatest dynasties in NFL history.

January 26, 1960—Pete Rozelle was named commissioner of the National Football League, replacing Bert Bell, who had died of a sudden heart attack.

February 9, 1960—The American Football League and National Football League made a verbal agreement not to "tamper" with another league's player while he was under contract.

January 1, 1961—The Houston Oilers defeated the Los Angeles Chargers 24–16, in the first AFL title game. A crowd of 32,183 watched the game.

April 5, 1961—The television and radio rights to the NFL championship game were sold to NBC for $615,000, with $300,000 of that money designated for the NFL Players Benefit Plan.

1962—The AFL made the scoreboard clock the official timer of the game, a rule the NFL copied soon afterward.

1963—Pete Rozelle suspended Green Bay halfback Paul Hornung and Detroit tackle Alex Karras for placing bets on their own teams and other NFL games. Rozelle also fined five other Detroit players $2,000 each, and fined the Lions $2,000 for "failing to report information promptly" and "lack of sideline supervision."

September 7, 1963—The NFL dedicated the Pro Football Hall of Fame at Canton, Ohio.

1963—Jim Brown set another NFL season rushing record with 1,863 yards.

December 29, 1963—The Chicago Bears beat the New York Giants, 14–10. It was George Halas's sixth league title in 36 years of coaching and playing.

1964—Cornell University kicker Pete Gogolak signed with the AFL's Buffalo Bills, becoming the first soccer-style kicker (kickers who boot the ball with the inside of the foot instead of with the toes) in the history of professional football. Twenty years later, conventional kickers would be obsolete.

April 5, 1965—The NFL changed the color of officials' penalty flags from white to bright gold.

December 29, 1965—CBS acquired the television rights to NFL regular-season games for $18.8 million a year.

April 7, 1966—Joe Foss resigned as AFL commissioner. Al Davis, head coach and general manager of the Oakland Raiders, was named to replace him.

1966—The St. Louis Cardinals moved into newly constructed Busch Memorial Stadium. Owner Charles Bidwill called it "one of the greatest football facilities in the world."

December 13, 1966—The NFL sold the television rights to the Super Bowl for four years to CBS and NBC for $9.5 million.

1968—The Houston Oilers left Rice Stadium to become the first NFL team to play inside a domed stadium, the Houston Astrodome.

February 7, 1969—Vince Lombardi became part owner, executive vice president and head coach of the Washington Redskins.

January 26, 1970—The NFL reached a deal with NBC and CBS for regular-season games. NBC agreed to televise all AFC games, while CBS agreed to televise all NFC games, with the exception of those played on Monday nights.

1970—The Pittsburgh Steelers moved into Three Rivers Stadium, and the Cincinnati Bengals moved into Riverfront Stadium.

September 3, 1970—Vince Lombardi died of cancer at the age of 57.

November 8, 1970—New Orleans Saints kicker Tom Dempsey kicked a game-winning 63-yard field goal against Detroit, setting a record that still stands. Amazingly, Dempsey was born with only one hand and half of a right foot.

Boyd Dowler of the Green Bay Packers gathering in a Bart Starr touchdown pass in the 1967 NFL championship game. The Packers won, 21–17.

March 25, 1971—The Boston Patriots changed its name to the New England Patriots and moved into Schaefer Stadium, which has been renamed Sullivan Stadium. Several other NFL teams moved into new homes: The Eagles moved to new Veterans Stadium, the 49ers moved into Candlestick Park and the Dallas Cowboys moved into Texas Stadium.

December 25, 1971—Garo Yepremian kicked a 37-yard field goal to lift the Miami Dolphins to a 27–24 playoff victory over the Kansas City Chiefs. The winning kick came after 22 minutes and 40 seconds of overtime. The overall game lasted nearly 83 minutes making it the longest game in NFL history.

April 5, 1973—The NFL adopted a jersey-number system: 1–19 for quarterbacks and specialists; 20–49 for running backs and defensive backs; 50–59 for centers and linebackers; 60–79 for defensive linemen and interior offensive linemen other than centers; and 80–89 for wide receivers and tight ends.

1973—O. J. Simpson of the Buffalo Bills became the first player in history to rush for more than 2,000 yards in a single season. He finished with 2,003 yards.

February 27, 1974—Pete Rozelle was given a new 10-year contract.

1975—The Detroit Lions moved into the new Pontiac Silverdome and the Saints moved into the Louisiana Superdome. The Giants moved into Giants Stadium in East Rutherford, New Jersey.

July 23, 1975—The Pittsburgh Steelers defeated the College All-Stars, 20–10 in the last game of the annual series. The game was shortened due to heavy rainstorms.

1975—Referees wore wireless microphones for the first time.

November 20, 1977—Walter Payton of the Chicago Bears set a single-game rushing record with 275 yards on 40 carries against the Minnesota Vikings.

1978—The NFL began a study on the use of instant replay as an officiating tool.

March 16, 1979—NFL officials were ordered to whistle a play dead quickly when the quarterback was clearly "in the grasp" of a defensive player.

The rule was designed to protect quarterbacks.

1979—The Los Angeles Rams moved to nearby Anaheim, California, but kept "Los Angeles" in their name.

1982—The NFL signed a five-year contract with the three television networks for all regular-season and post-season games starting with the 1982 season. The contract was worth $2.076 *billion.*

May 7, 1982—The Oakland Raiders won a lawsuit, enabling them to move to Los Angeles for the 1982 season. They changed their name to the Los Angeles Raiders.

March 28, 1984—In the middle of the night the Baltimore Colts loaded their gear into trucks and moved to Indianapolis. Owner Robert Irsay blamed the move on the "lack of cooperation" by the city of Baltimore in building a new stadium. The Indiana Hoosierdome became the Indianapolis Colts new home.

1984—A number of NFL records were set and broken. Miami Dolphins quarterback Dan Marino passed for a record 5,084 yards and 48 TDs. Los Angeles Rams running back Eric Dickerson rushed for a record 2,105 yards. Washington Redskins wide receiver Art Monk caught 106 passes. Chicago Bears running back Walter Payton broke Jim Brown's career rushing record, finishing the season with 13,309 yards.

March 11, 1986—The owners agreed to "limited use" of instant replay as an officiating tool. And in a new rule called the "Jim McMahon Rule," the NFL said players could not wear a personal message of any type on their game uniforms. McMahon, the Chicago quarterback, was known for putting messages on his headbands.

March 15, 1987—The NFL reached new three-year television deals with NBC, CBS and ABC for more than $1 billion. ESPN became the first cable network to carry NFL games when it reached an agreement with the league to carry eight Sunday night games.

October 31, 1987—Eric Dickerson, the greatest single-season running back in NFL history, was traded from the Rams to the Colts for six draft choices and two players.

March 14, 1988—NFL owners allowed the St. Louis Cardinals to move to Phoenix, Arizona. Owner Bill Bidwill, who assumed ownership of the

Brent Jones of the San Francisco 49ers is upended by a defender in 1988 playoff action.

team after the death of his brother, blamed the move on the "antiquated, dilapidated conditions" of Busch Stadium.

March 22, 1989—NFL Commissioner Pete Rozelle announced his retirement after 19 years on the job.

April 18, 1989—Tex Schramm was named president of the new Worldwide American Football League, an international arm of the NFL scheduled to begin play in the early 1990s.

August 31, 1989—The International League of American Football, founded by Carroll Huntress, announced it would begin play on April 14, 1990 in Europe. The ILAF stated it would place teams in England, Finland, France, West Germany, Italy and Spain. Each team would have 12 American players and 24 nationals. Joe Haering, a former NFL assistant coach, was named director of football operations.

CHAPTER 3
EQUIPMENT

SOCKS ON YOUR HEAD?

College and pro-football rules require that players be "properly and legally equipped at all times." College rules require that a player wear a jersey with numbers, knee pads, helmet and mouthpiece. Pro rules require a jersey with numbers, pants, helmet and socks.

What about shoulder pads? Or shoes? Of course, a referee would kick you out of the game if you didn't have on shoes (unless you're a barefoot kicker!). But not wearing the *right* equipment is just as foolish as not wearing shoes. Without the proper equipment, a player can be seriously injured. In this chapter we will review how and why equipment came about, and what is right and wrong for all types of players.

Imagine if you saw Boomer Esiason playing football with nothing but a stocking on his head! That sounds crazy, but in the early days of the game, that's all players wore because most players believed that growing their hair long would protect their skulls. It didn't work, and a lot of headaches resulted.

Most football equipment was developed in response to the changing requirements of the game. Shinguards were worn before 1900 because the rugby-style of football often caused severe injury to the shins. Cleats were invented in the early 1900s to help players run on slick or muddy fields. Logical, huh?

Around that same time, players began wearing leather helmets, and they sometimes stuffed padding into oversize shirts and pants. As the game evolved, so did protective equipment. But some players didn't like it. "Equipment is for sissies," Bobby "Night Train" Layne, a great quarterback for the Steelers in the 1950s, once said. But by 1960 all players were required to wear helmets, pants, shoulder pads, jerseys and cleats. With more modern equipment, players were able to protect themselves better. When a long career can mean millions of dollars, it is critical to protect every inch of your body as completely as you can.

Colts running back Eric Dickerson, for instance, wears a lot of equipment: helmet; goggles; mouthpiece; cage facemask; neck brace; gloves; shoulder pads; back, rib and stomach protection; bicep, forearm, hip, thigh, knee and shin pads. "There is nothing glamorous about injuries," says Dickerson. Being well-protected doesn't mean you're a coward. It means you're smart.

This peek underneath the standard football uniforms shows just some of the padding typically worn by NFL players.

THE HELMET— ARMOR AND WEAPON

The helmet is the most important piece of equipment a player wears. There are several types. All helmets are made of a hard, plastic-like substance, but the kind of padding used inside varies greatly. Some helmets are filled with air or liquid padding. Others are filled with soft padding. The most comfortable, according to a number of professional players, is the air-filled helmet. It can be pumped up, like a football, to fit your head. And when you run into something, the helmet "gives" like a shock absorber.

A helmet must be a perfect fit, or you will probably be in trouble. Why? Because a loose helmet can be slammed down on your face, resulting in a broken nose. Or if it's too tight, you will get horrible headaches and earaches, and might suffer serious injury.

When you try on a helmet, first wet your hair. Then you will know what the helmet will feel like when you're sweating. It should be very snug, but not painful. Professional players grab their facemask and move the helmet sharply from side to side. If the helmet moves, but your head doesn't, the helmet is too loose. If your head moves *with* the helmet without pain, then it fits. Remember—if you have a cheap head, buy a cheap helmet.

Football players used to brag that they didn't need helmets. But today's helmets are more than protective devices—many players use them as weapons. Jack Tatum, a former defensive back for the Oakland Raiders, once called his helmet "the great equalizer." He meant that no matter how good an opponent was, he could stop him by ramming his helmet into him. It is illegal in football to butt, ram or spear an opponent with the helmet. (To "butt" with the helmet means to slam an opponent with the forehead. To "ram" means to intentionally use the helmet to inflict pain. To "spear" means to dive at a falling ballcarrier with the top of the helmet, thus "spearing" him with the helmet.) But still it happens, sometimes unintentionally.

The standard pro helmet, with face mask and chinstrap

THE FACE MASK—YOUR NOSE WILL THANK YOU

The face mask is made up of plastic bars that fit on the front of the helmet. There are many different styles. Most linemen wear a "full-cage" mask, because they are involved in a lot of tackles and collisions and need the most protection. Quarterbacks, receivers and running backs prefer a smaller mask that allows them to see clearly. The mask should not obstruct forward or peripheral vision.

The face mask provides critical protection for the nose, eyes and mouth. If the opening in the part of the face mask that's in front of your eyes is too wide, a fist or foot could slip between the bars and break your nose or split your lip. Miami quarterback Dan Marino's full-face version protects his entire face. The opening around his eyes is too narrow for anything to slip in, and extends far below his chin and mouth. It doesn't obscure his vision, either.

SHOULDER PADS — BIGGER DOESN'T ALWAYS MEAN BETTER

Shoulder pads are made of slick plastic that is padded on the inside with either foam or air. They protect the shoulders, collarbone and chest bone. Some players used to believe that the bigger the padding, the better the equipment. That's not always true.

It is important to know your position before picking out a pair of shoulder pads. Quarterbacks

use a smaller, less restrictive type of pad. This gives them more freedom of movement when throwing the ball. Receivers, like Minnesota's Anthony Carter, also use smaller pads. If your pads extend too high above your shoulders, you can't turn your head. If you are a defensive back or receiver, it is important for you to be able to look behind you. Linebackers, who depend on quickness, must be careful not to get bogged down by their equipment.

Linemen, however, like Green Bay's Tony Mandarich, wear huge shoulder pads. Their job is to block and tackle, and they are involved in heavy collisions on every play. In that case, bigger *is* better.

If your shoulder pads are too small, they will pinch your neck. If they are too loose, they will slide, rub and move under heavy contact. This can cause blisters, sores and of course, pain. The pads should completely cover your shoulders and come down at least to the top of your biceps.

THIGH AND KNEE PADS

Thigh pads are made of hard plastic that is coated with a soft, foamy material. They wrap around the front of the thigh to absorb the shock of a tackle. They

Taping the hands—commonly done by players to avoid injuries

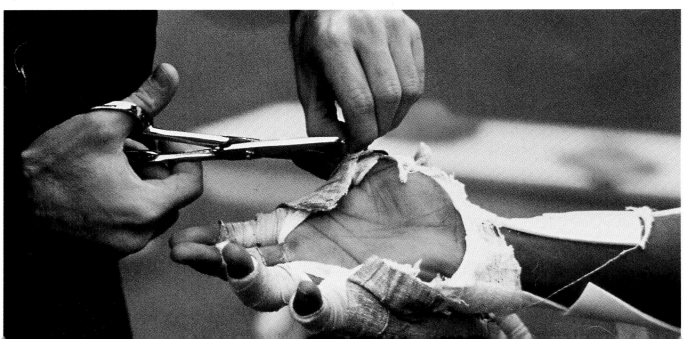

vary in size. Knee pads are normally made of thick, flexible foam. When both thigh and knee pads are in place in a pair of tight game pants, they should fit snugly and almost touch. Your pants should be snug but comfortable, with ample room for all your pads.

Linebackers, linemen and running backs whose legs take a lot of punishment, normally wear the thickest thigh and knee pads they can find. Certain companies make high-tech thigh pads, like those worn by the Houston Oilers defense end Ray Childress, that protect from serious thigh injuries. But the players most commonly hurt in the thigh area are the ones who fail to protect themselves properly. Many wide receivers will use the lighter, softer, knee pads instead of thigh pads, thinking it makes them a little quicker. That may be true. But the first time somebody rams into their upper legs at high speed, they will miss the protection of a big, thick thigh pad.

Knee pads shouldn't be taken for granted, either. Running back Marcus Allen of the Raiders removes his completely, in the belief that it makes him faster. But players can avoid serious bruises and injuries by wearing their knee and thigh pads. Knee pads cannot keep you from a serious knee injury, but they can help you avoid the serious nicks, scrapes and bruises that are common in the game of football.

The best and safest hip pads are worn in a girdle. A girdle is made out of stretchy material, with pockets for hip pads and a butt pad, which protects your lower spine. Once the pads are pushed into each pocket, they are very secure. You then step into the girdle and pull it up like a pair of shorts. Your game pants fit over the girdle.

DON'T BUY SHOES FOR THE AUTOGRAPH

It seems every shoe manufacturer pays a superstar to endorse and wear its shoes. Minnesota Viking running back Herschel Walker wears a certain shoe, Buffalo Bills quarterback Jim Kelly wears a certain shoe. But what is most important is finding the right shoe for you. Shoes that are too tight or too big can

Never far from the action, a team's equipment manager stands ready with mouth guards, tape and more.

HIP, HIP, HOORAY!

Thomas "Hollywood" Henderson was a linebacker in the mid-1970s for the Dallas Cowboys. He was running downfield on a kickoff when a blocker collided with his hip at high speed. "He hit me so hard it sounded like a gunshot," Hollywood says. Henderson never wore hip pads, because he thought he was "tough enough" to play without them. But that serious blow forced him to reconsider.

Hollywood suffered what is known as a hip pointer. When the hip gets a direct hit, it becomes inflamed. It feels like three or four bee-stings in the same place and hurts like that for days. That is why hip pads are so important.

cause blisters. There are turf shoes, grass shoes, and dozens of different styles of cleats. Turf shoes are different from grass shoes. Grass shoes have long rubber cleats attached to the bottom, which offer great traction on dirt, grass or mud. Turf shoes are covered with dozens of tiny rubber studs that "bite" into turf, which is harder than natural grass. In the early days of football, players mostly wore sneakers. But various field conditions led to more inventive ways for players to keep their footing.

Don't lace your shoes too tight—this will hurt your feet. Sometimes a bandage will help minor cuts or scrapes on the feet. Always wear two pairs of socks for added protection.

Jock of Ages

One of the oldest pieces of equipment is the jockstrap. It is designed to support your most sensitive area, the groin. Believe it or not, most professional players *do not* wear protective cups! But the cup, which is made of hard plastic, can prevent serious groin injuries. Players often joke that the guys who don't wear cups "have never been hit where it hurts." All it takes is one time!

Gloves, Tubes and Other Equipment

Every athlete is different. Like Eric Dickerson, some players prefer to protect every inch of their body. Other players, like Marcus Allen, wear little protection. But whatever you choose to wear, it's out there. "The best thing about sports today," says Dickerson, "is that good equipment is available to all players, even kids." This is true. Most sporting goods stores either stock or can order the same equipment worn by the pros.

The best way to be fitted properly for equipment is to know what feels right. If a helmet doesn't fit, don't wear it. If pants don't fit, don't wear them. Learn what feels comfortable by trying on as many pieces of equipment as you can. See what feels good and what doesn't. A lot of your equipment decisions will be made based on what position your coach asks you to play. After playing a few games, you will learn where you get hit the most.

Sometimes the most practical equipment is the simplest and cheapest to obtain. There are rubberlike tubes made of Neoprene that can be pulled up over the forearms and elbows. Presto! No scrapes, cuts or abrasions on your elbows or arms, and they cost less than $20. Receivers can be helped by wearing leather gloves with a sticky surface.

Pain Is a Friend, Not an Enemy

One thing every player must remember is that football is rough. "If you don't like physical contact," says Pittsburgh quarterback Bubby Brister, "then you're in the wrong game." No matter how much protection you wear, it can't keep you from feeling pain. Football requires toughness and courage. Proper equipment helps you get through minor bumps and bruises so you can concentrate on running, throwing and tackling. When you are equipped properly, a good hit makes you feel good all over. The contact may make you afraid at first, but the more you play, and the better you protect yourself, the more you'll enjoy it.

SECTION II:

IN THE HUDDLE

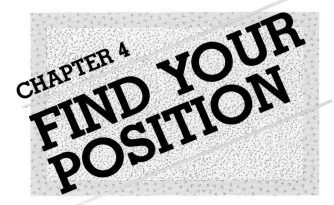

CHAPTER 4

FIND YOUR POSITION

LEARNING THE GAME

To appreciate football you must first understand the purpose of each position. Once you know the job of everybody on the team, you can really start enjoying the strategy behind the game. There are 22 positions—11 on offense and 11 on defense. Offense is very organized and orderly. The offense knows what play is going to run and where the ball is going. Coaches design plays they think will work against the defense. The quarterback then carries out the coach's orders. "Offense is like war," said Hank Stram, a former NFL coach. "It's a disciplined attack. You attack their weaknesses."

Defense is organized, too, but in a different way. On defense, players can be more reckless. They watch the offense and react to what they see. It takes great instincts and great reactions to play defense. Another important part of playing defense, though, is physical. The player must be able to slam down the ballcarrier or knock over blockers.

THE GUYS WITH THEIR SHIRTS HANGING OUT

The only players who line up in the same place on every play are the offensive linemen. There are five linemen on *every* play. They are usually big, husky guys with their shirts hanging out of their pants. Offensive linemen look sloppy because they block and battle the defensive line for an entire game. The offensive line creates holes for the running backs and protects the quarterback. Every lineman must be very strong and powerful. It also helps to be cocky. You must believe that you can overpower the guy across from you. You can't be afraid.

The Giants and the Vikings, nose to nose

In 1989 the Houston Oilers had one of the best offensive lines in football: Bruce Matthews, Dean Steinkuhler, Jay Pennison, Mike Munchak and Bruce Davis. The Oilers offensive line fought so much that their fans called them "The Bad Boys." They even wrote a song about them:

> *If you're looking for trouble*
> * You came to the right place*
> *If you're looking for trouble*
> * We'll put it in your face*
> *We're only made out of*
> * Flesh, blood and bones*
> *If you're gonna start a rumble*
> * You won't be all alone*
>
> *We're the Bad Boys*
> * Our middle name is misery*
> *We're the Bad Boys*
> * We're gonna bring you to your knees*

It helps to have a bunch of big, bruising guys up front. Without them, the offense couldn't run a single play. Some players think that if they get "stuck" on the offensive line, the coach doesn't like them. That's not true. Many times a team's best players are linemen. It is a position that requires speed, strength, coordination and a willingness to work hard. It also takes pride and dedication to be an offensive lineman.

The center is the man who snaps the ball to the quarterback. He has to be very quick, because he must snap the ball *and* block. Mike Webster of the Kansas City Chiefs played center in the NFL for 15 years. He has been the best center in football.

The guards line up on either side of the center. They are the most mobile, and the fastest, of all the linemen. On some plays they pull out—moving sideways instead of blocking straight ahead. Chris Hinton of the Indianapolis Colts is an example of a great guard. He pulled out on sweeps to block for Eric Dickerson. Anyone who got in his way got crushed.

33

The tackles line up outside the guards. They are the biggest of the offensive linemen. They block mostly straight ahead. Joe Jacoby of the Washington Redskins is a great big, physical tackle.

Pro linemen use several different blocking techniques. On running plays, they generally shoot out and block straight ahead. On passing plays, they step back and form a protective pocket around the quarterback. *How* they block depends on several things. If a lineman can physically control his opponent, he will "lock him up," or hook the defensive player under his shoulder pads, and drive him into the ground. When a lineman slams his man down, that is referred to as a "pancake." It takes great strength to pancake a grown man. When Green Bay's Tony Mandarich was at Michigan State, he had more than 100 pancakes in his college career!

If a defensive player is much bigger or faster than the offensive lineman, then some linemen may choose to block him *below* the waist. When the defensive man charges, the offensive lineman hurls himself at his legs. If done properly the defensive player is "cut" straight to the ground like a tree. This is very painful, however, and many defensive players get very, very angry when they get cut-blocked, as this move is called. It is easy to hurt someone accidentally with this type of block. During the 1989 season New York Giants linebacker Lawrence Taylor was the victim of a cut block. The Giants were playing the

San Francisco 49ers on Monday Night Football when Taylor was cut by a San Francisco player. Taylor's ankle and knee were severely sprained. The Giants started a fight with the player who hurt Taylor. The cut block is legal, but because it is so dangerous most players consider it a cheap shot.

On passing plays, most pro offensive linemen use a "punch" technique. With both hands open and arms extended, they punch the defensive player in the sternum area, then back up a step, which is called a shuffle step. When the defensive player charges again, they punch and step back again. The purpose is simply to stay between the defensive lineman and the quarterback. Offensive linemen must protect their quarterback at all costs.

HALF BLOCKER, HALF RECEIVER

Tight ends are sometimes called "tweeners," because they are stuck between being an offensive lineman and a wide receiver. They must be big enough to block, but quick enough to go out for

The Giants Mark Bavaro tries to run his way through a tackle. Bavaro is considered one of the top tight ends in professional football.

passes. And, of course, they have to be tough. One of the best is Philadelphia's Keith Jackson. He is 6′ 4″ and weighs 250 pounds. He is strong enough to take on defensive linemen, and so speedy he catches lots of passes.

These players are called "tight ends" because they line up tight on one end of the offensive line (see illustration). Whichever side the tight end lines up on is called the "strong side." The side opposite the tight end is called the "weak side." Pro teams run 60 or 70% of their plays to the strong side, because the tight end offers more blocking.

Tight ends block the same way as offensive linemen. Sometimes they have to block linebackers, who are quicker than defensive linemen. The best way to block a linebacker is to use the "cut" technique, even though it may hurt. Some tight ends, though, are strong enough to handle any linebacker nose to nose.

The Minnesota Vikings wide receiver Anthony Carter finds room between two defenders to gather in a touchdown pass.

SPEED BURNERS

Wide receivers line up wide on either side of the offensive line. They must be able to run fast, catch and block occasionally. But speed is very, very important. Receivers "stretch" the defense. They must force the defense to cover the entire field. The other team must keep guys deep in the middle of the field to keep the wide receiver from running past them. This creates other passing and running lanes for other receivers and backs.

Wide receivers are usually smaller than most of the other players on the field, but they must be *extremely* tough. Receivers often get tackled very hard after catching a pass. Houston's Ernie Givens got hit so hard once after a catch that he was completely flipped over.

Receivers must be disciplined, too. Defensive backs try to "jam" them (stop them) at the line of scrimmage by hitting them hard in the chest. Receivers have to fight off the jam and then run good routes that will beat the defensive players who are covering them. But speed isn't everything. Seattle's Steve Largent was not very fast. He just ran perfect routes, and he could fool the defense. He would pretend to be running one direction, then stop quickly and go another way.

His discipline and practice made him one of the best receivers in NFL history.

SLUG-MOUTH FOOTBALL

Teams ordinarily use two running backs. Usually, one is big and powerful, and the other is a little smaller, faster and shifty. The big back is called a fullback. The quick back is the tailback. Together they comprise a team's offensive backfield.

The fullback blocks more than he runs the football. He usually clears a path for the tailback.

Tailbacks vary in size. Some are as big as fullbacks but can run as fast as a receiver. Others weigh less than 190 pounds. But no matter what size they are, all tailbacks are explosive. They have the ability to accelerate past a tackler, the strength to run over people and the quickness to change directions. Some teams have great running attacks. Some coaches call running the ball "slug-mouth football" because there's nothing fancy—it's just you against them. The Kansas City Chiefs like to play "slug-mouth football."

Their tailback is Christian Okoye, who weighs an amazing 253 pounds. For a tailback, that is huge! But he is also fast. Okoye, who is from the African country of Nigeria, hits so hard they call him the "Nigerian Nightmare."

After receiving the handoff or pitchout from the quarterback, good running backs *always* protect the football. Rick Forzano, who used to coach the Detroit Lions, taught his backs this exercise to help prevent fumbles: You wrap your hands around the point of the ball, lock the other end of the ball into your elbow, and squeeze as tight as you can. This is called an isometric exercise; the word "isometric" refers to muscle contractions made against resistance. In this case the inflated football provides the resistance to the squeeze. Whenever you hear an NFL coach yelling, *"iso* the ball, *iso* the ball," he is telling his players to lock the ball in and squeeze.

Learning *how* to run with the football is very important, too. A good running back picks his knees up very high, almost to his chin. It's very hard for tacklers to grab his legs. If they don't get their arms completely around him, he will break the tackle. Running backs should be just as physical as the defense. Running backs catch passes on occasion, too.

THE PRETTY BOYS

Quarterbacks are often called the "pretty boys" of football, because so many great ones have been self-assured, stylish and good-looking. Quarterbacks aren't all style and no substance, however. They have to be good athletes, and also very, very tough. Pro quarterbacks get hit on almost every play, even when they don't have the ball.

The quarterback runs the offense. He makes sure everybody is lined up in the right place. The quarterback's job begins in the huddle. He must look around and make sure he has 10 other guys on the field. He has to be sure the right people are in the game. For instance, if he wants to throw deep to a certain receiver, he has to make sure the coaches remembered to put that guy in the game.

You would think that all good quarterbacks

Sometimes running backs must cope with another enemy— the weather.

have good arms, wouldn't you? But some of the greatest quarterbacks in history couldn't throw very hard. The great quarterbacks are accurate, however. They don't throw many interceptions. And they *don't* fumble.

Intelligence is very important, too. Quarterbacks must study their play books. They must be able to recognize anything the defense does to trick them. They can't get too excited during a game. They have to stay calm under any situation. When picking out a quarterback, coaches look for leadership and determination. Confidence comes from practice. But how they play in a game is the biggest test. "There are only two types of quarterbacks," said Darrel "Mouse" Davis, the offensive coordinator of the Detroit Lions. "One gets better when you put him in a game, the other gets worse."

It's been said that the quarterback gets too much credit when a team wins, and too much blame when a team loses. That is true. No matter

RAGING BULLS

Now let's talk about defense—the guys who try to stop the offense. Let's start with the defensive line. Most pro teams play with either three or four down lineman, as they are called because they lean down over the field with one hand touching the ground. They are typically very big and very fast. These guys can be brutal. They fight, scratch, claw, bite—whatever it takes to get to the football. Like the offensive line, they spend all their time fighting blockers. They are trying to sack the quarterback or make the tackle. Sometimes a team positions a defensive lineman directly opposite the center. In this situation he is called a nose tackle.

Defensive ends are the two players on the end of the line. They are usually the lightest of the front four, weighing anywhere from 250 to 275 pounds, and they are lightning-fast. The tackles, who are in the middle of the line, are usually bigger, sometimes weighing more than 300 pounds. The defensive linemen must watch the ball very closely, so as soon as it is snapped, they can charge.

Defensive linemen use several techniques to beat their man (the man they're covering). One is the "bull rush." A bull rush is a straight-ahead charge, like an angry bull would make. This bull rush is just man on man, tough on tough. The strongest man will win. Another technique is the "swim move." On the swim, the rusher pushes the blocker off with his left hand, then brings his right hand over the top, as if he's swimming past him. This move can be very hard to stop. Even if they don't get to the quarterback, defensive linemen can still be effective by raising their hands and knocking down the pass.

TRAINED KILLERS

The Houston Oilers refer to their linebackers as "trained killers." Linebackers are not really killers, and they're not really linemen, but they are bigger than defensive backs. They line up behind the defensive line.

how good the quarterback is, it still takes the entire team to win a game. A quarterback may be a great passer, but somebody has to catch those passes, right?

The main job of the quarterback is to outthink the other team. If the defense is expecting a run, he should call a pass. He also thinks about "setting up" the defense, or making them guess wrong. For instance, if the quarterback runs two running plays in a row, the defense will then tighten up in the middle, bunching together to defend against the run. Then he could call a pass play on the next play. The quarterback must always do the unexpected.

Even when they're sitting on the bench waiting to go back in the game, quarterbacks must be thinking about what they should do next. The quarterback must believe that, in every situation, he can somehow win the game. His teammates look to him for the leadership and confidence it takes to win.

Quarterback Dan Marino of the Miami Dolphins stands over the center and barks out the play.

one man to beat (see illustration). So if he is very quick, he is hard to block.

As we mentioned earlier, linebackers get cut-blocked a lot. That's why they should always play with their arms extended in front of them and their hands open. Linebackers have to fight off blocks, run around blocks and get to the football.

SMALL BUT SPEEDY

The modern defensive back is extremely fast, and a brutal hitter. Over the last 10 years defensive backs have gotten smaller and faster, primarily because the wide receivers they cover have gotten smaller

It is a position where brawn is essential, but brains mean more. Linebackers must be fierce competitors and savage tacklers. They must punish running backs and quarterbacks, and show no mercy on wide receivers. Linebackers try to intimidate other players.

"From the first day of practice, I could always tell who my linebackers were," says Joe Haering, a former NFL coach with the New York Jets. "I'd take my best defensive players and smack them in the head. The ones that smacked me back were linebackers."

If size and strength are critical, speed is essential. The great linebackers are also savvy and have great technique. They must see and recognize plays before they happen—like the few inches' difference in a running back's stance that could determine a run or a pass, or spotting a nervous glance that signals what play is going to be run.

In the past, even great linebackers like Pittsburgh's Jack Lambert didn't rush the quarterback the way they do now. These days a team's best rusher may be a linebacker. The great outside linebackers of today can toss an offensive lineman like a rag doll and still get to the quarterback.

A lot of teams use a 3–4 defense, with three down linemen and four linebackers. The weakside linebacker (who lines up on the side that doesn't have the tight end) usually only has

Minnesota quarterback Fran Tarkenton (#10) throws from a perfectly formed pocket.

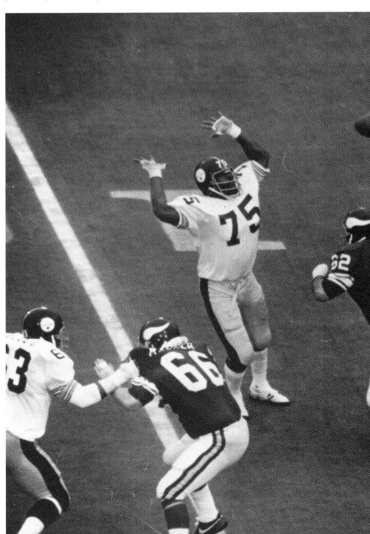

and faster. In a normal situation there are usually four defensive backs. As a unit those four guys are called the secondary. The area they cover is called the defensive backfield.

The fastest of the four defensive backs are usually the two cornerbacks. Cornerbacks are usually about 5′ 10″ or 5′ 11,″ and weigh between 190 and 200 pounds. Safeties are usually a little bigger and stronger than the cornerbacks. The weak safety lines up on the weak side. The strong safety lines up on the strong side, the same side as the tight end. The strong safety is responsible for covering the tight end, so he must be the biggest and strongest defensive back.

Defensive backs are usually heroes or goats. If they bat down a long pass or intercept a pass, everybody loves them. But if they are beaten out for a touchdown, everybody boos them. It takes great confidence to play defensive back. "You can't worry about what people think," says San Francisco's Ronnie Lott. "You just go out and do the best you can."

Linebacker Jack Lambert of the Pittsburgh Steelers doing what linebackers do best

HIT MEN

You've probably never heard of Ron Wolfley. Among the long list of stars in the NFL, Wolfley is not a household name. Wolfley, a fullback for the Phoenix Cardinals, usually just blocked and tackled on kickoffs and kickoff returns.

That doesn't sound like much. But Wolfley became so good at blocking and tackling on special teams that he went to the Pro Bowl three times. Special teams are the units that take the field when a team is switching from offense to defense. Punt teams, punt return teams, kickoffs and kickoff returns—those are called *special* teams.

And they *are* special. "I believe that I can make a difference in a game, just like Dan Marino," Wolfley said. "I can make the block that helps the return man score a touchdown, or I can make the hit that forces a fumble." The players on special teams are usually the craziest, hardest-hitting players a team has. Wolfley, for instance, shaved his head and wore several earrings in his left ear. And he was one of the most physical football players in the NFL.

Against Buffalo one year, he hit a linebacker so hard he knocked *himself* unconscious. But a few minutes later he went back in the game—and knocked himself out again! Obviously, it takes

39

special guys to play on special teams. "There's no feeling like running down the field as fast as you can," Wolfley says. "You hear all these horrible grunts and slams and bangs. Bodies are flying and feet are stomping. Then you find the guy with the ball . . . and knock his brains out."

Ouch!

But hitting people isn't the only important thing about special teams. It is important to have a kicker that can kick the ball high and long on kickoffs. High kicks allow your players to run down the field before the other team has a chance to run it back. Kickers also can win games with field goals. This too makes the kicker very important.

Punters are also important. On the fourth down, they must kick the ball as far as possible. The object of punting is field position. You always want the other team as far away from your goal line as possible. That's why long punts are critical. But when the other team is punting or kicking a field goal, you want your special teams to block it. The Houston Oilers blocked six punts in one season, which tied an NFL record.

But it is the fierce collisions that make special teams so much fun to watch. When two professional players run into each other at full speed, the impact could move a Boeing 737 airplane an inch!

The New York Giants Willie Anderson shows how close a defensive back must play if he is to break up pass plays or, better yet, snare an interception.

CHAPTER 5
STRATEGY

Now that you understand what everybody on a football team does, let's talk strategy. Strategy is figuring out how to beat the other guys. Football is like chess. You have to outthink the other team. The best way to win a game is to put your strength against their weakness. For instance, if you have a good wide receiver, you have to figure out how to get him matched up with their worst defensive back.

There are basic formations that every team utilizes. Out of the formations we discuss in this chapter, you could literally run thousands of plays. Every NFL team hires up to a dozen assistant coaches to help teach the players what they should do. The biggest part of coaching is teaching. First there is the head coach. The head coach makes the final decision on every call. Then you have a coach for each position: wide receiver, quarterback, running back, offensive line, tight end, defensive line, linebackers, and secondary.

Coaches shouldn't just boss their players around. Nobody likes a coach who says, "Do it because I said so." A coach should explain *why* a play works. Then he should make his team do it over and over in practice. That is called repetition.

Another key to strategy is *personnel,* the people you have on your team. You have to pay attention to the kind of play you have. For instance, if you have four fast wide receivers, you want to throw the ball more. If you have a great running back, you should run the ball more. In the early 1970s Don Shula took the Miami Dolphins to the Super Bowl behind the power running of Larry Csonka and Jim Kiick. In 1984 when the Dolphins had Dan Marino, they threw the ball more than any other team in football.

The head coach is responsible for picking out the right players and finding talented new play-

ers each year. Every year the NFL holds a draft where college players are "drafted" or chosen by NFL teams. In the draft, each team is allowed 12 selections. The team with the worst record during the previous season gets to pick first. The next worst team is second, and so on, down to the Super Bowl champion, which is the last team to draft. After the draft any player who wasn't picked is free to try out with any NFL team. A lot of good players, like Chicago quarterback Mike Tomczak, never get drafted.

After a coach looks at all his players, he must figure out the best place to play them. Roy Green, the Cardinals speedy wide receiver, was a defensive back in college. His coach switched him to wide receiver in the pros, and he became one of the best in the NFL. The most aggressive players usually end up on defense. Coaches like players with courage and leadership. "I look for leaders on offense, defense and special teams," says Chicago coach Mike Ditka. "And I hate cowards and losers."

Now that a coach has looked at his players and figured out where to put them, he decides on what formations the team will run. Keep in mind that there are dozens of formations. In this chapter we will discuss the most common ones.

The San Francisco 49ers quarterback Joe Montana gets some information from the team's "spotters"—the men who sit at broadcast-booth level and analyze the game from above.

OFFENSE: THE PRO SET

The pro-set offense is the most common offense in the NFL. It has the five basic offensive linemen, a tight end, and a wide receiver split to either side. The quarterback lines up behind the center. If the fullback and tailback line up next to each other, this is called a split backfield. If the tailback lines up behind the fullback, this is called the I-formation.

Keep in mind that the only players who are eligible to catch a pass are those either in the backfield or at the very end of the line of scrimmage. In the pro-set, one of the wide receivers lines up on the line of scrimmage. He is sometimes called the split end. The wide receiver on the same side as the tight end is called the flanker. He lines up a yard back from the line of scrimmage, which puts him in the backfield. If the flanker lined up on the line of scrimmage, it would make the tight end ineligible to catch a pass because he would no longer be at the very end of the line of scrimmage. Sometimes the flanker goes in motion, or runs in a straight line behind the quarterback before the ball is snapped.

Why do players go in motion? Because the defense doesn't know where he is going. This con-fuses the defense and helps the offense do different things. Out of this basic formation, the offense can do many different things.

Now let's design a play out of this offense. Every pro team has its own numbering system for calling plays. First they number the areas outside and between the offensive linemen. Then they number the backs, quarterback, fullback and tailback.

Every team is different, but this is an example:

(1) SE (2) LT (3) LG (4) C (5) RG (6) RT (7) TE (8)
QB (1)   FL

FB (2)

TB (3)

Using this numbering system, let's continue designing our play. Say it's second down and inches to go for a first down. We want the flanker to go in motion to the left. Then we want to run the tailback behind the block of the right guard. The fullback will be the lead blocker. This means he will charge into the hole ahead of the fullback. So this is what our play would sound like in the huddle:

"Load Dive right thirty-six, on two."

Here's what the quarterback said: "Load" told the flanker to go in motion to the left. "Dive right" told the team that the primary direction of

The basic quarterback drop with two running backs in position

the play was right. The number "36" meant that the number 3 back, the tailback, will carry the ball through the number 6 hole, or right off the guard. "On two" meant the ball would be snapped on the second hut. Here's what the play looks like on paper:

```
   X
                X               X       X
X          X  X  X  X  X  X
SE         LT LG C  RG RT TE
                QB                  FL
                FB
                TB
```

See? That's not too hard. Of course every team has its own terminology. Every team numbers and names things differently. But almost every team runs similar plays. A few years ago, there was a great quarterback named Fran Tarkenton who played for the Vikings. He was traded to the New York Giants. The same week he was traded, he played in a game. He didn't know the Giants' terminology, so he would call a play in the huddle by simply saying "fullback dive right," or "flanker screen."

Almost every NFL team uses some style of the pro-set offense. As we said it can look different on every play because sometimes they use two tight ends and only one receiver, or even three tight ends and no receivers.

Washington Redskins John Riggins finds a gaping hole in the Miami Dolphin line.

THE RED GUN

The fastest way to move the ball in the NFL is with the pass. It is also the most exciting way to play football. Nothing is more fun than to watch the quarterback scramble around like crazy and then throw a perfect 30-yard pass for a touchdown. NFL teams have designed formations that give great quarterbacks the best chance to utilize their talent.

In passing situations most NFL teams use a four wide-receiver system. They take out one running back, usually the tailback, and take out the tight end. Then they replace them with two speedy receivers. Here's what that formation looks like:

WR   LT LG C RG RT   WR
        QB
   WR WR
        FB

Many times one of the wide receivers lined up in the backfield will go in motion. Once the play begins, the offensive line pass protects (protects the players involved in the pass), as does the fullback. The four wide receivers then run various routes in an effort to get open. The Houston Oilers call their four-receiver formation the Red Gun. A lot of teams, including the Oilers, will line up in the "shotgun" formation on obvious passing downs. Here's an example of the shotgun formation :

WR   LT LG C RG RT   WR
   WR WR
       QB   FB

Notice that the only difference in the shotgun formation is that the quarterback lines up in the backfield next to the fullback. This gives the quarterback a chance to look up and see the defense before the snap. It also gives him more time to throw if a team is putting on a severe pass rush. Houston, and a few other teams, occasionally hikes the ball to the fullback, not the quarterback. That confuses the defense because they think it's going to be a pass. Instead the fullback takes off running.

On passing plays out of any formation, wide receivers run basic routes (see illustration below). On a fly pattern they run straight down the middle of the field as fast as they can. On a slant pattern, they slant over the middle. On an out pattern the receiver runs hard at the defensive back, then breaks to the outside.

The two most important pass routes are the post and flag. On a post the receiver runs downfield, then breaks toward the goal*post*. On a flag he runs, then breaks outside toward the *flag* markers at the corner of the end zone. Fast receivers get open on these two routes more than on any others.

Basic Pass Routes

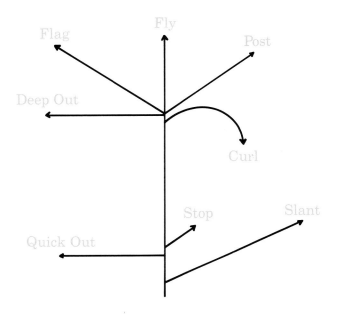

THE MOUSE THAT ROARS

A lot of coaches believe that the Run 'n' Shoot offense is the future of the NFL. The man behind the revolution of the Run 'n' Shoot is a coach named Darrel "Mouse" Davis, who stands just 5' 9". Davis invented the Run 'n' Shoot offense while coaching high school football in Portland, Oregon, in the 1960s. Today he is an assistant coach with the Detroit Lions. Parts of his offense are used by more than a dozen teams around the NFL.

The first thing you notice about the Run 'n' Shoot is that there are *always* four wide receivers, regardless of down and distance, and that the football is *always* in the air. Here's the way it looks:

```
WR          LT LG C RT RG          WR
  SB              QB          SB
  (WR)                        (WR)

                  TB
```

Davis's offense spreads a defense so thin that there simply aren't enough men to cover everybody. On every down, the offense posts a receiver on each sideline, and a "slotback" outside each tackle. All four receivers—who are required to be very fast—read the defense and react. For instance if a defensive back is playing a receiver inside, he will break outside. If he's playing him outside, he'll break inside. And so on.

The quarterback rolls out on each play, which means he moves to his right or left as he drops back. He must read the same situations the receivers do. So regardless of how the defense plays, the receivers "run where you ain't," Davis says.

One slot goes in motion on every down. The single running back is responsible for backside pressure—that is, the defensive pressure that comes from a quarterback's blind side, the side opposite where the play is going. He may also loop out into pass routes, or carry the ball on occasion. There is never a tight end. Remarkably, the playbook consists of just eight basic plays: three running and five passing.

Sounds crazy, doesn't it, when passing is so popular in the NFL? Yet since 1962, when Davis first made his invention public, no offense on record, including the old wishbone and veer formations, has experienced the success of the Run 'n' Shoot. Davis's high-school quarterbacks *routinely* threw for more than 300 yards. His teams won four league championships and made the playoffs seven times. Davis spent six years at Portland State University, where his teams won by scores of 105–0, 93–7, and 75–0 and set more than 20 college records.

At first, high school, college and professional coaches said the Run 'n' Shoot was doomed to failure. But in 1977 Mouse discovered a great quarterback in Neil Lomax, who played for Mouse at Portland State (PSU). Under Lomax, PSU led the nation in scoring three times. The Run 'n' Shoot averaged 49.2 points *per game.* In four seasons Lomax fired 106 touchdowns and surpassed 300

yards 40 times. Once, against Delaware State, Lomax completed 12 of 18 passes for 254 yards and 7 touchdowns—in the first quarter. "I threw touchdowns to every receiver on the roster," recalls Lomax.

Detroit Lions wide receiver coach June Jones also played quarterback for Davis at Portland State. His lanky build, drooping mustache, curly black hair and crooked eyeglasses made Jones look more like a handyman than a coach. At Portland State, Jones rode the Run 'n' Shoot to national prominence, setting an NCAA record for most yards passing—3,463—in a single season. He was drafted by the Atlanta Falcons, where he played six years.

Randall Cunningham of the Philadelphia Eagles, equally good at passing, scrambling and rushing, is a classic run-and-shoot threat.

Jones and Davis both coached with the USFL's Houston Gamblers in 1984. The Gamblers had Jim Kelly, a rookie quarterback with a strong arm. Behind the Run 'n' Shoot, Houston established new all-time, single-season American professional marks for points (618), total yards (7,684), passing yards (5,311) and touchdown passes (79). In two seasons Kelly threw 83 touchdowns. Jones and Davis's success helped revolutionize the offensive schemes of the NFL.

It took Mouse 27 years to break into the NFL. But now his offense is widely used throughout the NFL and in major colleges. Mouse Davis has been credited with the major success of the University of Houston, where the Run 'n' Shoot has made the Cougars the Number 1 offense in the nation. Houston quarterback Andre Ware won the Heisman Trophy in 1989, thanks to a man called Mouse. About a dozen NFL teams—including Cincinnati, New Orleans, Pittsburgh and the New York Giants—use portions of the Run 'n' Shoot. June Jones, before he went to the Detroit Lions, installed the Red Gun offense with the Houston Oilers.

"You can't have a 'do it because I'm the coach' philosophy," says Mouse. "What we do requires more discipline than any other offense. Being able to think for yourself and make the right decision—that's discipline. I believe you can accomplish anything if you just want it bad enough, and you're willing to sacrifice what it takes to get there."

Perhaps the Run 'n' Shoot will someday change the way the entire NFL plays offense.

DEFENSE: A WALK ON THE WILD SIDE

The job of the defense is simple: Stop the other guys and get the football back. In the next few pages we will discuss the various methods NFL coaches use to do just that. Unlike offense, where you start out with basic formations and build from there, the defense must react to what the offense does. Down and distance also dictates how the defense will line up.

In the early years of professional football, teams used a 5–2 alignment which put pressure on the quarterback but left the center of the field wide open. The 4–3 came about in the mid-1950s, when a coach decided to let one man—who wasn't big enough to play defensive line—drop off and play the middle. This led to the 4–3 defense, which is still used often today.

This continued until 1971 when defensive masterminds Bill Arnsparger of the Miami Dolphins and George Allen of the Washington Redskins began tinkering with what many thought was perfection. Allen devised the "nickel" coverage—removing a linebacker on passing downs in favor of a fifth (five cents, get it?) defensive back. Arnsparger, meanwhile, used a fourth linebacker

A sideline defensive huddle

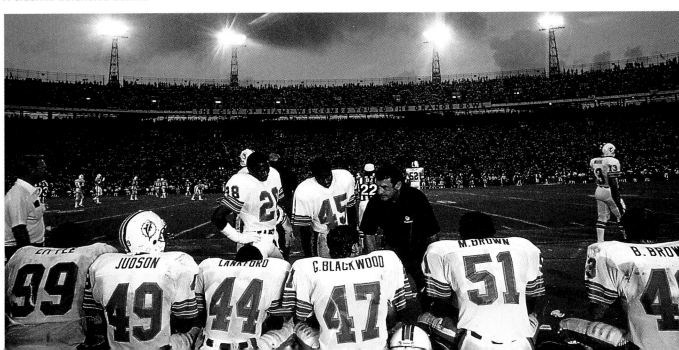

Short-yardage situations often create pile-ups at the line of scrimmage. Here a linebacker or defensive back tries to stop a leaping running back.

the modern 3–4 defense, and with it came a new breed of linebacker, the "tweener" like the Giants Lawrence Taylor or Green Bay's Tim Harris. Players like this cause severe problems for the offense. They can line up and cover wide receivers or tight ends, or they can play down on the line and are strong enough to take on an offensive tackle.

Here's the way it works. Coaches like the 3–4 defense on obvious passing downs. This way they can insert extra linebackers or defensive backs to cover people. If the offense puts in four wide receivers, the defense will put in five defensive backs. That's called "nickel" coverage. If the defensive uses six defensive backs, that's called "dime" coverage. Seven defensive backs is "quarter" coverage.

The 4–3 defense puts an extra lineman on the line of scrimmage. If you were playing against a very good quarterback, you would probably play a 4–3 defense so you could put more pressure on him and force him to hurry his throws and make mistakes. Most teams prefer to play man-to-man coverage in the secondary.

SMASH-FACE FOOTBALL

Football is most physical when one team has the ball on the goal line or needs only a couple of yards for a first down. More than likely the other team will try to slam the ball up the middle. This means bodies flying and helmets cracking. This is muscle on muscle. "Goal-line football is smash-face football," says Pepper Rodgers, a former pro coach. "That's how you separate the men from the boys."

On short-yardage or goal-line defense, coaches will usually put eight players on the line of scrimmage and three players just a few feet behind them. The linemen "submarine" the offense line. Submarine means they dive at their legs in an attempt to knock them down. This allows the three other guys to dive over the top to get the man with the ball. Most of the time the strongest guy wins in short-yardage situations.

No-Passing Zone

In a long-yardage situation a defense will often play a zone defense. Instead of covering a man, they cover an area. The defense will usually rush just three people with everybody else dropping back and watching the quarterback to see where he throws the ball. Once he throws it, the defense swarms to that area. Here's an example of a zone defense; the dashes that form a circle indicate the general area that player must cover.

Because the defense knows you need a lot of yards for a first down, they will let you make a five-yard catch or a seven-yard catch. They just don't want to give up a lot of yards. "Keep everything in front of you," coaches will say. What the coach means is that if you keep the ball in front of you, you can run up and make the tackle. But if a man gets behind you, he could outrun you for an easy touchdown.

It was January 1980. The Pittsburgh Steelers were playing the Los Angeles Rams in the Super Bowl. The winners would be world champions. Late in the game the Steelers were winning 24–19. But the Rams were driving fast. In 7 quick plays, they moved from their 16-yard line to the Pittsburgh 32.

The Rams decided to trick the Steelers. Los Angeles quarterback Vince Ferragamo took the snap and stuck the ball in the stomach of his running back. It looked like a running play. But instead of giving the running back the ball, Ferragamo kept it and turned to throw! It was a fake run! He threw the ball over the middle toward his receiver.

But out of nowhere, Pittsburgh linebacker Jack Lambert jumped up and intercepted the pass. He was the only Pittsburgh player who hadn't been fooled by the fake run. Why? Because Jack Lambert knew how to read *keys,* which is what you are about to learn in this chapter.

This lineman is watching the play develop, looking for clues he can use to stop the ball.

READING KEYS

What Lambert noticed before the play was that the Rams offensive linemen were leaning *backward,* not forward. "Just before the snap, one of their offensive linemen had his butt too high," Lambert explained later. "His weight was on his heels." Think about that for a second. If a team was going to run the ball, the linemen should be leaning *forward,* so they could fire out and block. But if they were going to block for the pass, they would lean back on their heels so they could back up and protect the quarterback. So Lambert *knew* it was a pass because of a lineman's butt! A lineman's butt may have made the difference in the Super Bowl—the Steelers went on to win.

WHITE KNUCKLES, NERVOUS EYES

Coaches call it "reading keys" because you learn to "read" the habits or actions of other players that may tell you what is about to happen. Once you figure out what is going to happen, then you have a "key" that will unlock the other team's secrets.

Here are some examples. One time Doug Williams, the quarterback for the Washington Redskins, was playing in an important game. But every time the Redskins ran a play, the defense seemed to know it ahead of time. When Williams passed, the defense was in perfect position to cover. When he handed off, the defense swarmed the offense. His team lost the game.

The next day Williams watched the game on film. Guess what he discovered? Every time his team *ran* the ball, Williams *didn't fasten his chin-strap,* because he knew he wouldn't get hit on the play. But whenever it was a passing play, he *would* fasten his chin-strap, because he knew he might get tackled. "It was a stupid mistake," says

Williams. But the defense noticed, so they knew what Williams was going to do.

Tony Dorsett, who was a great runner for many years with the Dallas Cowboys, once made a similar mistake. When the Cowboys would line up before a running play, Dorsett would jiggle his face mask. "It was just a bad habit," Dorsett says. But whenever the defense saw him jiggle his face mask, they knew he was about to carry the football.

Offensive linemen are the easiest to read. Pittsburgh offensive tackle Tunch Ilkin admits that he gives away plays all the time. "I can't help it," he says. "I've tried to stop, but I keep doing it." What Ilkin does is very similar to the guilty Los Angeles Rams linemen in the 1980 Super Bowl. On passing downs he leans back. On running plays he leans forward. But many offensive linemen do that. The best way to tell is to look at the hand that he has down on the ground. If his knuckles are white, it means he's leaning forward. What is he going to do? Run, of course. If he doesn't have any weight on his hand, it's probably going to be a pass.

Sometimes a quarterback may see something on defense that he's not prepared for. In that case he can audible—shout out a different play while standing over the center—or call timeout and regroup, like Cleveland Browns Bernie Kosar is doing here.

49

SENDING A MESSAGE

A lot of players "telegraph" plays with their eyes. You send someone a message by telegraph, and that's exactly what happens when somebody telegraphs a play. For instance a wide receiver will nervously check the area where he is about to go out for a pass. Read? *Pass.* A running back looks over at a hole right before the play, to see how the defense is lined up. Read? *Run.*

Even great players like quarterback Bernie Kosar make mistakes. On running plays Kosar often lines up with his feet next to each other. But on passing plays, he will line up with his right foot back so he can drop back to pass quickly. Buffalo quarterback Jim Kelly sometimes turns around and checks the position of his running backs before a running play. On passing plays he will check the position of each wide receiver.

The best way to learn to read keys is to watch a lot of football. Keep a notebook of all the "keys" you discover. Who knows—you may be able to spot the key play in a Super Bowl before it happens!

SECTION III:

▼ ▼ ▼ ▼ ▼

WEEKEND WARRIORS

▲ ▲ ▲ ▲ ▲

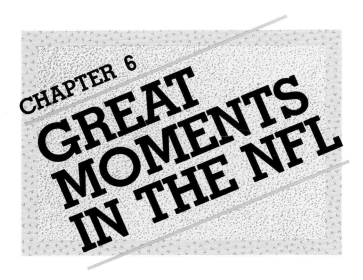

CHAPTER 6

GREAT MOMENTS IN THE NFL

WHO ARE THE CRYBABIES NOW?

It all started near the end of the 1940 NFL season when the Washington Redskins met the powerful Chicago Bears. The Bears, led by coach George Halas, were a great team. They had the best quarterback in football, Sid Luckman. They also had the NFL's best runner, George McAfee. The Redskins had passing quarterback Sammy Baugh. But despite the talent of the vaunted Bears attack, the Redskins upset them, 7–3, just a few weeks before the NFL playoffs. The Bears complained after the game that the referees hadn't been fair and that they should have won the game.

The newspapers quoted George Preston Marshall, who owned the Redskins at the time, as saying that the Bears were "nothing but a bunch of crybabies." There was no doubt the two teams hated each other after that. And only two weeks later the Redskins and the Bears would meet again for the NFL championship.

George Halas was a smart coach. He studied films of the Bears' loss to the Redskins and figured out a perfect plan to beat Washington. He also put in a bunch of new plays that the Bears hadn't used in their first game with the Redskins. Then Halas cut out the headlines about the Redskins calling the Bears "crybabies" and hung them in Chicago's locker room. This got all his Bears growling mad.

The NFL championship was scheduled for December 8, 1940. It was a warm and sunny day, and a crowd of 36,004 turned out to watch the game. Just before the kickoff, players from both teams got into an argument. "There was a lot of tension in the air before the game," said Chicago quarterback Sid Luckman. "You just knew something tremendous was about to happen."

It took less than one quarter for "something tremendous" to happen. On Chicago's first play, Luckman handed off to fullback Bill Osmanski, who slammed off left tackle, burst out into the open and ran 68 yards for the touchdown. The Redskins came charging back but were forced to punt. Then the Bears marched 80 yards in 17 plays for another touchdown. They didn't throw the ball, they *banged* the ball down the throats of the famous Washington defense. When the Redskins stalled again, the Bears scored *another* touchdown. It was 21–0 at the end of the first quarter.

Washington could do nothing right. The Bears intercepted passes for touchdowns. They returned punts for touchdowns. Luckman completed long passes for touchdowns. In the second half, Chicago scored 7 touchdowns, rolled up 382 total yards, and intercepted *8* Washington passes. The final score was 73–0, an NFL record that still stands today.

As the players walked off the field after the game, Sid Luckman couldn't help gloating. "Hey," Luckman yelled at the Redskins, "who are the crybabies now?"

THE HORSE

If somebody ever tells you that "you aren't good enough" to play football, just think of Johnny Unitas. Unitas was a ninth-round draft choice of the Pittsburgh Steelers in the early 1950s. But the Steelers, who already had three quarterbacks, cut Unitas. When the Baltimore Colts finally signed him, he was playing semi-pro football for the Bloomfield Rams for $6 a game. All Unitas did was step in, and through hard work and determination, he became the NFL's Most Valuable Player in 1957.

Despite Unitas's early success, he still wasn't too well known by the time of the NFL championship game in 1958. The Colts had many weapons:

Washington Redskins running back Jimmy Johnson (in dark jersey) draws a crowd of Chicago Bears. Neither Johnson nor his teammates made much progress in this 1940 game.

The final score: Bears 73, Redskins 0. Note the face mask-less helmets!

Baltimore Colts running back Alan Ameche lowers his head and booms into the end zone for the winning touchdown against the New York Giants.

wide receiver Raymond Berry, running back Alan "The Horse" Ameche and defensive superstars Gino Marchetti and Gene "Big Daddy" Lipscomp. But when the Colts invaded New York's Yankee Stadium to play the Giants for the NFL title, most fans believed the Giants would win the game.

The Giants had beaten Baltimore during the regular season, and Baltimore hadn't beaten the Giants since 1954. The Giants were led by quarterback Charlie Conerly and wide receiver Frank Gifford. It was truly a battle of "giant" proportions. A crowd of 67,175 fans packed Yankee Stadium to witness what was at that time the biggest game in NFL history.

Early in the first quarter the game was a punting duel. Neither team could pick up a first down. The Giants finally broke the deadlock when kicker Pat Summerall kicked a field goal from Baltimore's 36-yard line. But minutes later in the second quarter, Frank Gifford fumbled and Big Daddy recovered inside the 20-yard line. With Unitas calling the plays, Ameche, "The Horse," finally slammed it in for the touchdown and the Colts led, 7–3.

With the first half winding down, Gifford fumbled again. Baltimore took advantage of Gifford's slippery hands and marched the ball 70 yards before Unitas hit Berry with a 15-yard touchdown pass. The Colts were ahead 14–3 at the half.

Early in the third quarter Unitas went for the kill. He marched the Colts down to the New York three-yard line. Four times Ameche smashed into the line, only to be pushed back by a courageous New York defense. Then the Giants got the ball back on their own two-yard line. Excited after such a tremendous goal line stand, New York rallied. Four plays later, running back Mel Triplett scored for the Giants, making the Colts lead 14–10.

The defenses of both teams settled in, forcing several punts. Finally Frank Gifford redeemed himself with a 15-yard touchdown catch early in the fourth quarter, which put the Giants ahead, 17–14. Meanwhile darkness was settling in and cold winds were sweeping the stadium. After two more Baltimore drives ended in punts, New York fans sensed victory as the Giants began to run out the clock.

With just minutes to play, Gifford ran off tackle on third down and 4 yards to go at the New York 40-yard line. Gino Marchetti and a host of Colts met Gifford head-on at the first-down marker. It was a fierce collision, but it looked as if Gifford had made it. Marchetti was taken from the field with a broken leg. When they sorted out the pile of players, Gifford was short. The Giants had to punt.

Baltimore took over at its 14-yard line with 1:56 to play. The Giants fans were screaming, but

Unitas wouldn't die. He completed pass after pass, shredding the New York defense. With 7 seconds remaining in the game, the Colts had moved to the Giants 13-yard line. Kicker Steve Myhra kicked a field goal, which tied the score at 17–17.

The game went into overtime, *the first overtime in NFL history.* The team that scored first would win.

Somehow Baltimore had managed to regain its momentum, despite the loud hooting of the New York crowd. The Colts held the Giants on their first series in overtime. Baltimore took over on their 20, and Unitas coolly went to work. He marched the Colts forward on an 11-play drive. During that drive, Unitas calmly hit three passes for first downs, including a sideline shot to tight end Raymond Berry, who went out of bounds on the one-yard line.

The crowd was at full roar when Unitas ducked into the huddle and called a dive play to The Horse. The two teams lined up. Several million people watching the game on black-and-white TV were glued to their screens. Unitas took the snap and handed the ball to Alan Ameche. Ameche lowered his head as he entered the heart of the New York defense.

Touchdown! The Colts had won the championship! To this day, many believe that game was the greatest championship in football history.

A SHINING STARR

There were just 13 seconds showing on the clock. It was December 31, 1967, and the Dallas Cowboys and Green Bay Packers had battled down to the game's last play for the right to the NFL championship title. Both teams were exhausted. And both teams were very, very cold.

The temperature had dropped to 13 degrees *below* zero. Several players suffered frostbite during the game. At half time the band couldn't play—it was so cold that the trumpet player's lips stuck to his instrument. The field in Green Bay had frozen over, so the playing surface was like concrete.

Quarterback Bart Starr (#15, center) followed his blockers into the end zone for the winning touchdown in the 1967 NFL championship game against the Dallas Cowboys.

Early in the game Green Bay quarterback Bart Starr had completed touchdown passes twice to wide receiver Boyd Dowler, giving the Packers an early 14–0 lead. But the Cowboys, behind their "Doomsday Defense," fought their way back into the game. Time after time Starr was smeared by Dallas linemen. Eight times he was sacked as the Cowboys turned two fumbles into a touchdown and a field goal. Then in the fourth quarter, the Cowboys took the lead for the first time with a 50-yard option pass from half-back Dan Reeves to wide receiver Lance Rentzel.

But Starr and his frozen Packers mustered the strength for a final drive. Trailing 17–14 with 4:54 to play, Starr marched the Packers 68 yards in 12 plays to the Dallas 1-yard line. Twice Starr handed off to tailback Donny Anderson, who hammered into the vaunted Dallas defensive line. Twice he was thrown back for a no gain. There were just 13 seconds to play. "We had run out of ideas," Starr explained later. "The footing was real poor, the field was covered with ice. We were stumped for something to do."

On third down and goal, Starr took matters into his own hands. The called play was supposed to be a dive by fullback Chuck Mercein. But at the snap of the ball, Starr saw a tiny crack in the line

next to guard Jerry Kramer, so he put his head down and charged! There was a huge pileup on the goal line. Starr had made it across the frozen line by inches!

The Packers won 21–17. It was their third NFL championship in a row, the first time any team had won the league title three consecutive times. It also gave the Packers the right to play in the first Super Bowl against the Kansas City Chiefs, champions of the new American Football League.

MIAMI'S CHRISTMAS MIRACLE

The 1971 NFL season was highlighted by the Miami Dolphins and their strange cast of characters. Their running backs, Jim Kiick and Larry Csonka, called themselves "Butch Cassidy and the Sundance Kid," because they were a little bit like outlaws. They had refused to play until the team paid them a higher salary. And they had run over most of Miami's opponents.

The Dolphins quarterback, Bob Griese, had established himself as a star too. Throwing deep spirals to receiver Paul Warfield, the upstart Griese quickly became feared around the league. But the most unlikely Dolphin star was their little kicker, Garo Yepremian. Yepremian had been making neckties before he signed on to kick field goals for the Dolphins.

The Kansas City Chiefs had dominated the NFL that season with such noted stars as quarterback Len Dawson, running back Ed Podolak, receiver Otis Taylor and linebacker Willie Lanier. When the Chiefs lined up to play Miami on Christmas Day 1971, for the American Football Conference title, most fans thought they would quickly defeat the Dolphins. The Chiefs would then go on to play in the Super Bowl.

To no one's surprise, Kansas City started with a bang, scoring a field goal and a touchdown in the first quarter. But Griese answered with a long touchdown drive. Larry Csonka ran over Lanier for a two-yard touchdown. Late in the first half little Garo kicked a field goal to tie the score.

Kansas City took over again in the second half.

Gary Yepremian's 37-yard field goal sails through the uprights to give Miami a 27-24 win over Kansas City in the NFL's longest game ever.

Behind Dawson the Chiefs marched down the field against the Dolphins defense, taking 9 minutes before they scored again to lead, 17–10. But Griese refused to give up. On Miami's next drive Griese threw four passes—and completed all of them. The last pass went to Jim Kiick, who barreled over the goal line. Yepremian made the extra point and the game was tied, 17–17.

But Kansas City wasn't finished, either. The Chiefs wide receiver Elmo Wright took the ball 63 yards to the Miami 3-yard line, and Kansas City scored on the next play. Miami trailed, 24–17.

Once again Griese brought his Dolphins back from the dead. Twice they faced third and long, and twice Griese found an open receiver for the first down. Then Griese hit tight end Pat Twilley on the Kansas City five-yard line. On the next play, Griese saw his other tight end, Marv Fleming, crossing the back of the end zone. He fired. Touchdown Miami! The score was tied again 24–24.

There was a minute to play in regulation when Garo kicked off. Ed Podolak gathered in the kickoff and took off. Suddenly he broke into the clear. There was nobody left but tiny Garo! The kicker bravely hurled his little body at Podolak, who was forced to slow down and change direction. This slight adjustment slowed Podolak just enough for Miami's Curtis Johnson to drag him down and save the game. With the ball on Miami's 22-yard line, Kansas City lined up to attempt a chip-shot, a 32-yard field goal. Their kicker, Jan Stenerud, had been the best kicker in the NFL that season. Stenerud hit the ball with a thud. It looked good, but then it hooked right, missing by inches!

The Dolphins went crazy on the sidelines. They were still alive! The game went into overtime. The first team to score would win. The mighty Chiefs marched down the field again, and Stenerud lined up for another short field goal. Once again the ball thudded off Stenerud's mighty foot. But then there was another thud! The kick had been blocked by Miami linebacker Nick Buoniconti. The Dolphins had their second miracle of the game.

The game wore on. In overtime Garo got another chance, this time from 52 yards. He missed. "Just give me one more chance," he told his teammates. "I will kick it good next time." The fifth quarter ended and the game rolled into a *sixth* quarter.

Quarterback Bob Griese, who had played perfectly all day, went back to work. The call that would clinch the game wasn't a pass, but a run. Halfway into the sixth quarter, Miami had the ball on its own 35-yard line. Jim Kiick pounded for five yards. Then Griese entered the huddle.

"Roll right, trap left," he said.

It was a misdirection play, meaning it would start one way but come back the other way. It was designed to take advantage of the swarming Kansas City defense. Griese took the snap and stepped to his right. Csonka stepped right, took the ball, then charged back left behind guard Larry Little. Csonka rumbled all the way down to the Kansas City 36 before he was tackled.

Griese carefully maneuvered the ball down to the Kansas City 30-yard line in the middle of the field. Into the game came little Garo and his holder, Karl Noonan.

Noonan handled the snap perfectly and Yepremian's left foot hammered the ball. The exhausted players on both teams turned and watched as the ball tumbled through the black sky toward the uprights.

Good!

It was the NFL's longest game, 82 minutes and 40 seconds. The Dolphins won, 27–24, and were on their way to the Super Bowl. After the game Yepremian expressed his sympathy for Jan Stenerud, the Kansas City kicker who missed two field goals. "I feel very sorry for Jan," he said. "But I feel very happy for me."

THE IMMACULATE RECEPTION

In 1972 the Pittsburgh Steelers had existed for 39 years without a championship. Their owner, Art Rooney, had purchased the team for $100 back in 1933, and he had suffered through many losing seasons over the years. In 1969 his team won just one game in 14 tries. But Rooney had hired a new coach named Chuck Noll, and it appeared that Noll had the team heading in the right direction at last.

The Steelers finished 1972 with an 11–3 record and faced the vicious Oakland Raiders for the championship of the AFC Central Division. The Steelers were playing at home and thought they could pull off an upset.

But things didn't start that way. For the most part the game was an unspectacular defensive struggle. Both teams fought, scratched and clawed, which gave both offenses a hard time. Then a great run by Oakland quarterback Kenny Stabler put the Raiders ahead, 7–6, and time was running out.

With 22 seconds to play the Steelers faced the fourth down. Quarterback Terry Bradshaw dropped to pass. There was nobody open. As Bradshaw scrambled, fans began heading toward the exits. Rooney, the disappointed owner, got on an elevator that would take him down to the Pittsburgh locker room.

Running back Franco Harris races downfield along the sideline with the last-second score that gave Pittsburgh a win in 1972 playoff action.

But Bradshaw wasn't finished. He scrambled away from an Oakland tackler and fired the ball 40 yards downfield toward running back John Fuqua. Oakland defensive back Jack Tatum saw the ball in the air and ran toward Fuqua. Just as the ball arrived, Tatum hammered Fuqua, and the ball bounced high.

Art Rooney was in the elevator when he heard the Pittsburgh crowd go crazy. "What happened?" he asked the elevator operator when he got off outside the locker room. "I think we won!" the man screamed. "I think we won the game!"

The pass had bounced off Fuqua and was falling toward the turf when Franco Harris, a rookie running back, picked the ball off his shoetops and began running toward the end zone. Many Oakland players stood and watched in stunned disbelief. One Raider had a chance to stop Harris, but Franco ran through the tackle for a 62-yard touchdown with no time left!

The Steelers won the game, 13–7. And best of all, they were finally champions.

THE BLOOPER BOWL

The Super Bowl is supposed to be a match-up between the two best teams in professional football. But one year the championship turned into a comedy of errors in which a combination of mistakes and fluke plays made it one of the most memorable Super Bowl games in history.

Super Bowl V was played on January 17, 1971 between the Baltimore Colts and Dallas Cowboys. It was a much-awaited showdown between Colt quarterback Johnny Unitas and the Cowboys Doomsday Defense. But instead of a precision offense against a precision defense, the two teams played like clowns under a big top—every score was the result of a crazy mistake.

Halfway through the first quarter Unitas fired an errant pass that hit surprised Dallas linebacker Chuck Howley right between the numbers. Howley returned the interception to the Colt 46. Dallas punted, however, but Colt receiver Ron Gardin fumbled on the nine-yard line. Dallas recovered, and it looked as if they would score.

But on a third down Cowboy quarterback Craig Morton overthrew a wide open receiver in the end zone. The Cowboys kicked a field goal.

Dallas got the ball back and threatened to score again, driving the ball down to the Baltimore six-yard line. Then Morton threw the ball to an ineligible receiver, resulting in a 15-yard penalty. So Dallas's Mike Clark kicked another field goal, which made the score 6–0.

Baltimore got on the board by mistake. Johnny Unitas dropped back and fired a pass to receiver Eddie Hinton. But Unitas overthrew the ball, and it flicked off Hinton's hands. Dallas defensive back Mel Renfro dove for the ball, but it bounced off his hands, too. The ball skittered into the hands of Baltimore's John Mackey who grabbed it and ran 45 yards for the touchdown. The extra point was blocked so the game was tied at 6–6.

Moments before the end of the first half Unitas fumbled. Dallas recovered and scored again, putting the Cowboys ahead, 13–6. With just seconds left in the first half Unitas was hurt attempting to pass. He was replaced by Earl Morrall, who had little luck throughout the third quarter.

In the fourth quarter Colt Ed Hinton again was involved in a wacky play. Hinton caught a pass near the Dallas goal but Cowboy cornerback Cornell Green slapped the ball out of his hands at the end zone. The ball bounced around crazily as Cowboys and Colts alike dove madly for it. But the ball kept bouncing through everyone's hands and finally bounced off the field. It was ruled a touchback, and Dallas took over on their 20-yard line. Another Colt scoring opportunity had died.

Then Craig Morton threw an interception to Colt safety Rick Volk, who returned the ball to the Dallas three-yard line. Baltimore fullback Ed Nowatzke then slammed over for the score, and rookie kicker Jim O'Brien kicked the extra point. Super Bowl V was tied, and there were just two minutes to play.

Once again it was Morton who messed up. He went back to pass, and then was sacked for a 10-yard loss. Dallas got penalized for holding,

which moved the ball back to the Dallas 27. Morton tried to pass again, and the ball went through the hands of the receiver and into the arms of Colt linebacker Mike Curtis, who rumbled back to the Dallas 28-yard line.

The Colts tried two running plays, which gained three yards, then called time out with five seconds to play. Into the game came O'Brien, the

Baltimore kicker Jim O'Brien celebrates his game-winning field goal in Super Bowl V.

Quarterback Otto Graham of the Cleveland Browns carries the ball himself in the 1950 NFL title game against the Los Angeles Rams.

rookie kicker, who was called "Lassie" by his teammates because he had long hair. "Don't worry, Lassie," Morrall said. "Just kick it."

The teams lined up for the field goal. The Cowboy players were screaming and jumping up and down trying to distract O'Brien. The ball was snapped. Morrall placed it down on the 32-yard line. Several Dallas players dived to block the kick as O'Brien thumped the ball high into the sky. The ball tumbled crazily toward the goalposts.

The kick was good. Baltimore had won the "Blooper Bowl," 16–13.

WELCOME TO THE NFL

When the Cleveland Browns joined the NFL from the All-America Football Conference in 1950, many hard-line NFL teams made fun of the new team. Members of the Los Angeles Rams made fun of the AFC itself, calling it a "bush league, the minor leagues." But when the Browns wound up playing the Rams for the NFL title that year, nobody was laughing.

The Browns and the Rams, ironically, were very similar in style. Both teams were leaders in the modern passing revolution, and when they clashed for the league championship, the skies were filled with footballs. The talent of both teams was amazing. The Browns had three great receivers in Mac Speedie, Dante Lavelli and Dub Jones. The Rams countered with Tom Fears, flanker Elroy "Crazylegs" Hirsch and Glenn Davis.

"Instead of our running setting up the passing, our passing sets up the runs," said Hamp Pool, the Rams offensive coordinator. The Browns also believed in the pass as the best, most efficient way to move the football.

The game started with fireworks, which set the pace for the rest of the game. On the first play Rams quarterback Bob Waterfield connected with Glenn Davis for an 82-yard touchdown pass play. But Browns quarterback Otto Graham came firing right back, throwing a 31-yard touchdown minutes later to tie the game, 7–7.

This was just the beginning. Waterfield would wind up with 312 yards passing on the day, while

Graham finished with 298 yards and 4 touchdowns. What hurt Los Angeles was that Waterfield threw four interceptions on that afternoon.

The momentum seesawed back and forth, but the Browns were ahead just once, 20–14, in the third quarter. At that point the Rams scored 14 points in 21 seconds. Fullback Dick Hoerner dove in for a touchdown and then defensive end Larry Brink picked up a Browns fumble and returned for a score. The Rams led, 28–20, and appeared to be out of trouble.

But Otto Graham, who was having a brilliant day, wasn't finished. When no receivers were open, Graham tucked the ball under his shoulder and scampered for critical first downs. Finally with just minutes to play, Graham fired his fourth touchdown pass of the day. The Browns got the ball back on their own 32-yard line with 1:50 showing on the clock.

Graham coolly marched his team into field-goal range, ignoring the pressure of the fierce Los Angeles defense. With 28 seconds on the clock, kicker Lou "the Toe" Groza came on to try a 16-yard field goal.

It was good! The upstart Browns had won the NFL title! Waterfield said after the game, "They aren't bush league anymore." More important, both teams were exciting, zinging passes from end zone to end zone. It was a turning point for the NFL—professional football had truly become a thrilling spectator sport from start to finish.

THE MIRACLE THAT DIED

When the 1980 season began for the Miami Dolphins, there was much uncertainty over who the starting quarterback would be. At the end of the season veteran Bob Griese had become the 14th NFL quarterback to top 25,000 yards passing. But Griese, who had withstood his share of NFL beatings, retired, and rookie David Woodley became the starting quarterback in 1981.

Under Woodley the Dolphins finished with an 11-4-1 record and made the playoffs against the San Diego Chargers, who were known for their vaunted passing attack behind quarterback Dan Fouts. Both teams had explosive offensives, but their defensive units left much to be desired—especially Miami's defense, which found itself down 24–0 before the first *quarter* even ended.

Many Miami fans gave up and headed for the exits before halftime. But that was a big mistake, because before it was all over, this game would be one that the spectators would never forget.

Early in the second quarter Dolphins coach Don Shula replaced Woodley with veteran backup Don Strock. "Strock just seemed more appropriate at the time," Shula said later. "He was a veteran, and I knew that being down 24–0 would not bother him." Shula was right. Strock quickly took control of the game. He led a 63-yard drive that ended in a field goal, then threw a touchdown pass to Joe Rose.

Moments later, trailing 24–10, the Dolphins engineered the most exciting play in the game. Strock dropped back to pass and hit receiver Duriel Harris over the middle. As several San

Quarterback Dan Fouts of the San Diego Chargers in action against Miami in their 1981 divisional playoff game.

Diego Chargers rushed in to make the tackle, Harris spun around and pitched the ball to tailback Tony Nathan, who was trailing the play. As several stunned Chargers watched in disbelief, Nathan took the ball up the sideline for a touchdown! Miami had cut the lead to 24–17.

San Diego added to its lead with a 25-yard touchdown pass to tight end Kellen Winslow from Chargers quarterback Dan Fouts. But the Dolphins weren't through yet. Strock threw 2 more touchdowns, and at the start of the fourth quarter Tony Nathan ran 12 yards for another score. Amazingly, after trailing 24–0, the Dolphins led, 38–31.

But Fouts, who had passed for an NFL record 4,802 yards during the regular season, marched the Chargers back with an 82-yard drive. Time and again Fouts' passes found Winslow, who finished the game with 13 catches for 166 yards.

With 58 seconds to play in the game San Diego tied the game on a 9-yard pass to James Brooks, knotting the game at 38–38. Overtime!

After Miami missed a field goal attempt early in the overtime period, Fouts went right back to work. He marched the Chargers steadily downfield, then connected on a 39-yard pass to receiver Charlie Joiner. Finally place kicker Rolf Benirschke trotted onto the field. Thirteen minutes into the overtime period, Benirschke hit a 39-yard field gold to end the game.

It had been a record-setting game. Strock finished the game with 403 yards and 4 touchdowns, while Fouts threw for 433 yards and 3 scores. For the first time in NFL history both quarterbacks on opposite teams passed for more than 400 yards, and the two teams finished with more than 1,000 yards in total offense.

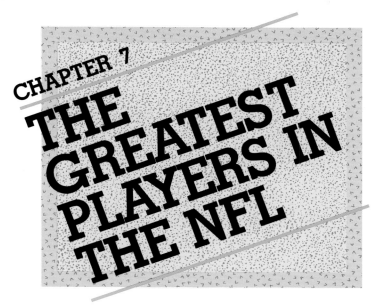

CHAPTER 7

THE GREATEST PLAYERS IN THE NFL

A LINEBACKER NAMED BISCUIT

The heart and soul of the Buffalo Bills defense is linebacker Cornelius Bennett. When he played for the University of Alabama, Cornelius was the first linebacker ever to win the Vince Lombardi Trophy. This award is given to the best lineman in college football. He has put fear in the hearts of opposing ball carriers. His teammates call him "Biscuit," because he likes to eat. At 6′ 2″ and 235 pounds, Bennett is the linebacker of the future. "I think Cornelius is incomparable as far as pursuit," says Marv Levy, Bennett's coach. "No linebacker in the world ranges from sideline to sideline like Cornelius Bennett."

The Buffalo Bills traded their 1988 first-round pick and 1989 first- and second-round picks to the Indianapolis Colts to get Cornelius Bennett. At the time some NFL coaches said the Bills had been buffaloed. But Bills general manager Bill Polian stands by his decision. "Cornelius, in his first full year [1988], helped take us to the division championship and the brink of the Super Bowl," he says.

Bennett, who signed a $4 million contract with the Buffalo Bills, earned every penny in his first full season. He was voted to the Pro Bowl after making 103 tackles and 9.5 sacks, and 2 critical interceptions. "He's got the whole package—strength, speed, intelligence and a love for the game," says Bills defensive coordinator Walt Corey.

THE IRON MAN

If Superman is the "man of steel," then San Francisco 49ers Roger Craig is the "iron man" of pro football. Running back is the toughest position in football, but Roger has never missed a game in seven violent years with the San Francisco 49ers. His knees-to-chin-strap running style punishes tacklers.

Roger spent most of his college days at the University of Nebraska as a backup to Heisman Trophy winner Mike Rozier. But since the 49ers made Roger the 49th pick overall in the 1983 draft, he has become one of the best backs in the NFL. Superstar quarterback Joe Montana and bruising fullback Tom Rathman share the 49er backfield. Together they make life miserable for an opposing defense.

Champion middleweight boxer Michael Nunn is Craig's brother-in-law. While Michael punishes opponents in the ring, Roger is a knockout on the field. He's been called the best all-around athlete in football. Desire and conditioning have helped him win two Super Bowl rings with the 49ers. Roger runs and lifts weights to stay healthy. "It's just like a car getting a tune-up," Roger says. "If

Linebacker Cornelius Bennett of the Buffalo Bills

TOO HARD-TO-HANDLE RANDALL

The University of Nevada, Las Vegas is known for its great basketball players. But Philadelphia discovered a UNLV *quarterback* who is teaching the Eagles how to run and gun. They call him "Too-Hard-to-Handle" Randall Cunningham, one of the NFL's most talented athletes.

He plays football as though it's basketball in shoulder pads, slinging passes to receivers like Keith Jackson and Cris Carter and scrambling through defenses for first downs. At Nevada, Las Vegas Randall became only the third quarterback in the NCAA to throw for over 2,500 yards in three straight seasons. The other two were John Elway and Doug Flutie.

An incredible runner, Cunningham has led NFL quarterbacks in rushing for three straight years. He looks skinny at 6' 4" and 203 pounds, but his strength and speed fool tacklers. "Cunningham is one of the toughest quarterbacks in the game," says Buddy Ryan, Randall's coach. Always a threat to score, Randall will gamble on his own talent to make the difference. Once when he was scrambling against the New York Giants, linebacker Carl Banks smashed hard into Cunningham. Randall started to fall, put his hand down and caught himself, then threw a touchdown pass. "The defense doesn't have any way of stopping him," Ryan says. "He just does it on his own...when he's scrambling around and makes one of those big plays, either running or throwing, that lifts the whole team."

Cunningham was the starting quarterback for the NFC in the 1989 Pro Bowl and was named the game's most valuable player. "Booster" organizations also praised Cunningham. He received the Maxwell Football Club's Bert Bell Award as the NFL Player of the Year in 1988. That same year the Washington Touchdown Club voted him the best in the NFC.

Randall is so good that he is the only quarterback in the NFL who gets to call his own plays. "A lot of people have been given talent from God, but they never worked at it," Randall says. "That's

Running back Roger Craig of the San Francisco 49ers

you don't tune it up, it's going to misfire. If it tears down, you have to rebuild it. That's how I approach my body."

The 49ers depend on 6-foot, 214-pound Craig's slashing style to carry their ground attack. But he's seen success through the air as well. In 1985 he became the first NFL player ever to gain 1,000 yards rushing and receiving in the same season. Roger is always among the league's best offensive players. Nobody expected Roger Craig to be so good. "But hard work always pays," Roger says. "You can have anything if you work for it."

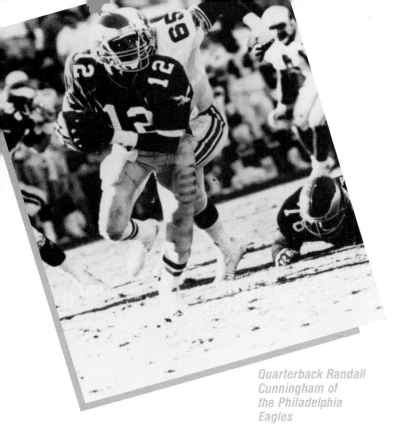

Quarterback Randall Cunningham of the Philadelphia Eagles

Bowls, and gained over 100 yards in 51 games. He's the only back ever to gain 1,000 yards in his first six years in the pros. His best single game effort covered 215 yards on 27 carries against Houston in 1984. That year he also rushed for an NFL record 2,105 yards in a single season.

Eric Dickerson, twisting and spinning for every available yard, is one of the NFL's greatest running backs. The 6′ 3″, 224-pound star has terrific ability and desire. "I don't play against other people," Eric says. "I play against myself. I know that I'm the best. So I have to prove that to myself every time I play." Eric has proved it so often that you can bet someday he will join other NFL legends in the Pro Football Hall of Fame.

why I work so hard, so God can see I'm not taking advantage of the situation in the wrong way. I want to be the best."

AWESOME ERIC

The Indianapolis Colts gave up three first-round draft picks, two second-round picks, and another player for Eric Dickerson, because they knew they were getting someone special. Eric won four NFL rushing titles in seven years. Only Eric, Walter Payton and Franco Harris have rushed for 1,000 or more yards in six straight seasons.

Just one word is needed to describe Eric Dickerson: awesome. His ability to spot the hole, pick up speed and burst into the defensive secondary make him the best runner in football. In college he starred at Southern Methodist University and rewrote the record books in the Southwestern Conference. His coach at SMU was Ron Meyer, who went on to coach Dickerson with the Colts.

Eric came to the pros with the Los Angeles Rams in 1983. His impact was immediate. He won every Rookie of the Year award in the NFL. In just six years he broke into the list of top-10 all-time rushers in pro football, started in five Pro

Running back Eric Dickerson of the Indianapolis Colts

ROCKY MOUNTAIN HIGH

ost NFL coaches are happy if their quarterback has a rifle arm. John Elway has a cannon. His accurate passing led the Denver Broncos to two Super Bowls in the 1980s. But his receivers know when the ball is thrown their way that it's coming hard. He throws the ball so hard that it bruises his receivers. They call their bruises "The Elway Cross," because the point of the football leaves a cross mark on their arms and stomachs.

Elway's favorite targets are Vance Johnson, Mark Jackson and Ricky Nattiel, better known as the "Three Amigos." Possibly the most talented pure passer in the NFL, Elway regularly throws for more than 300 yards in a single game. In 1988 he became the first player ever to throw for 3,000 yards and rush for 200 in four straight years.

John set five NCAA records during his college career at Stanford University, where his father, Jack Elway, coached. He was the first player selected in the 1983 draft. The Denver Broncos traded for John and signed him to a five-year, $6 million contract. The deal earned him the nickname of the "Six-Million-Dollar Man." Some might say that's too much to pay for one player, but the Broncos would disagree.

Looking downfield for an open receiver or slipping away from a tackler's grip, Elway is always a scoring threat. His teammates have voted him their most valuable offensive player four straight seasons. Like Randall Cunningham, Elway's ability to run and throw makes him one of the NFL's best quarterbacks.

Quarterback John Elway of the Denver Broncos

A BOY NAMED BOOMER

orman "Boomer" Esiason had his nickname before he was born. When Boomer was still inside his mother, he kicked around a lot. In football a good kicker is often referred to as a "boomer." "He must be a boomer," his father told his mom, "because he kicks so much." But Boomer's left arm would turn out to be much more dangerous than his legs.

The NFL's Most Valuable Player in 1988, Esiason has become one of the best deep passers in the NFL, with his tight spirals to receivers like Tim McGee and Eddie Brown. "He is a top performer," says his coach, Sam Wyche. "When he is at full strength, the team can count on him."

Boomer and the Bengals made it all the way to the Super Bowl in 1989 before losing to the San Francisco 49ers. Twice in his career, Boomer has passed for over 400 yards in a game. Boomer believes in setting positive goals, then working hard to achieve those goals. "I strive to have the Number-one offense in the league and to be the Number-one-rated quarterback in the NFL," he says.

The first quarterback picked in the 1984 draft, Boomer uses his size—6' 5" and 225 pounds—to its best advantage. Helping the Bengals win football games is Esiason's main concern. When Boomer won the NFL's MVP award, he shared his success with the rest of the team. "The Most Valuable Player is a funny award in a team sport," he says. "It's something to be proud of, but it's something that comes because of the other players around you. I realize how good the players are around me. They are the only way I could be named MVP."

Quarterback Boomer Esiason of the Cincinnati Bengals

intercepted five passes in a season. He has been to the Pro Bowl three times.

The Washington Redskins have played in three Super Bowls in the 1980s and Darrell Green's skill at cornerback is a big reason why. He has a talent for being in the right place at the right time. Green consistently makes the hit that knocks the football loose or closes fast to knock a pass down.

"Darrell is always matched against the opponent's big play receiver," says Richie Petitbon, the Redskins defensive coach. "He's going to give up some yardage, but his presence also stops big plays." And if a running back gets past the Redskins defensive line, it's a safe bet Green will chase him down. One time Green was playing against Eric Dickerson when Eric broke through on a long run. Green was on the other side of the field, but he was able to run Eric down. "Darrell was the first person to ever catch me," Dickerson says.

The Redskins depend on Green to make the big play. His interceptions and punt returns often set up key touchdowns for Washington. His experience helps him make the right decisions on the field and gives him a mental edge. But pure speed is what makes 5' 8," 170-pound Darrell Green one of the NFL's best.

Boomer is right. Football is a team sport. One player can make a difference, but it takes the whole team to win. That's why Boomer Esiason and the Bengals are winners.

THE NFL'S FASTEST MAN

Speed kills. Just ask Darrell Green of the Washington Redskins. He has won the "NFL's Fastest Man" competition—a contest held annually by the league's speediest players—three times. And what does he get for being so fast? Darrell always has to cover the other team's best receiver.

But Darrell loves the challenge. He's a master at playing pass defense and keeping the ball out of receivers hands. Twice in his career, Green has

Cornerback Darrell Green of the Washington Redskins

Linebacker Tim Harris of the Green Bay Packers

TERRIBLE TIM

Green Bay linebacker Tim Harris is fast becoming known around the NFL for his ferocious playing style. He is the main reason the Packers are playoff contenders again. Twice in 1988 against the Vikings, Harris sacked Wade Wilson in the end zone for safeties. In the Packers second meeting with Minnesota, Harris had five solo tackles, two sacks, then blocked a Bucky Scribner punt, caught the rebound in stride and returned it for the winning touchdown. "*Awesome* is the closest word," says an NFL scout. "He has a great move on the blitz and simply overpowers anybody in his way. You have to block him with a tackle. He'll kill a back."

His 13.5 sacks in 1988 were the 5th-best totals in the NFL, as Harris finished his 3rd NFL season with 83 solo tackles and forced a pair of fumbles. "On third downs, I look to myself to make the sack instead of asking someone else to do it," Harris says.

Last November against Chicago, Harris roared by All-Pro tackle Jimbo Covert and leveled quarterback Mike Tomczak, who left the game with a separated shoulder. "Harris is as good a defensive player as there is in the NFL," says Covert. "He's big. He can run. And when you watch a guy who has fun playing football, it's him."

Harris hopes his peers will reward him in 1990 with his first nomination to the Pro Bowl. Incentives in his contract will add an additional $70,000 to his $425,000 salary if he is selected.

"He runs people down with his speed," says his coach, Lindy Infante. "Harris is simply in a class by himself."

GO, BO, GO

Vincent "Bo" Jackson is blessed with natural ability. From April through October, he's an outfielder swinging a big bat for major-league baseball's Kansas City Royals. When the Royals finish their season, Bo just changes uniforms. Then he becomes a star running back for the Los Angeles Raiders.

Bo is just as comfortable ripping a home run over center field as he is running down the sidelines. Bo hit over 20 home runs in his first two seasons with the Royals. In 1989 he was awarded Most Valuable Player honors in baseball's All-Star Game.

Bo plays for the Raiders for only about half the football season. Even so, he electrifies the crowd with his moves. His best performance with the Raiders came on November 30, 1987, when he rushed for a club record 221 yards and 3 touchdowns at Seattle.

On that night he ran into Seattle linebacker Brian "the Boz" Bosworth. Bo and the Boz collided at the Seattle two-yard line with a crash. But Bo knocked Bosworth on his back and scored a touchdown. Until then fans had questioned whether Bo could really play both sports. But after that play, everybody—especially Bosworth— knew Bo Jackson was for real.

At 6′ 1″, 230 pounds, Bo was an All-America at Auburn University and won the Heisman Trophy in 1985. He was originally the first player taken in the 1985 draft, but he chose to play baseball instead. A year later the Raiders took a chance on him in the seventh round. Today he is the hardest-working athlete in sports. "Baseball," says Bo, "is what I love. Football is just my hobby."

Running back Bo Jackson of the Los Angeles Raiders

In college Jim beat out Bernie Kosar and Vinny Testaverde to set numerous records at Miami. He played two years in the United States Football League, which went out of business in 1985. In 1984 he was the USFL's most valuable player with 5,219 passing yards and 44 touchdowns.

In 1986 Jim, who is 6′ 3″ and 219 pounds, joined the Bills. During the 1988 season he brought Buffalo back from trailing 17–0 to a 34–23 win over the Colts. He finished the game with 315 passing yards and three touchdowns. The next week he completed 16 of 27 passes for 302 yards and 3 touchdowns against the New York Jets.

Kelly is often criticized by the fans because his statistics aren't that good. "The only statistic I count," Jim says, "is victories. As long as we keep winning, nothing else matters."

Quarterback Jim Kelly of the Buffalo Bills

A Lunch-Bucket Quarterback

Announcers often call Buffalo's Jim Kelly a "lunch-bucket quarterback." That's because he reminds people of a hard-working guy, like a construction worker who carries his lunch to work with him every day. Most NFL quarterbacks are flashy stars. But Jim Kelly is a linebacker in a quarterback's body. He is very physical. In one game when a defensive player hit one of his receivers, Kelly punched the linebacker in the mouth.

One in a long line of great quarterbacks from the University of Miami, Kelly is known for changing the direction of the Bills, who were in last place when he first signed with them. Kelly directed them to the AFC Eastern Division championship in 1988. His leadership and determination have motivated the entire team. Against Miami in 1989 he dove across the goal line on the game's last play to win the game. "I'm not pretty," he says, "but I get the job done."

Tim's strong play was a big reason for the Bengals reaching Super Bowl XXIII. But early in the Super Bowl, Tim Krumrie broke his leg in two places. It took him nearly a year to recover from the injury. But Krumrie worked for hours every day to rehabilitate the injury. When the 1989 season opened, Krumrie was back in there.

Seattle Seahawks coach Chuck Knox calls Krumrie "the finest nose tackle in the NFL, bar none."

His own coach, Sam Wyche, said, "Week in and week out, he's one of the best nose tackles in football."

Tim Krumrie is another great player whose road to success started in his own imagination. He believes in himself and understands that being the best isn't easy. "I'm confident in my ability," he says. "I'm going to work that much harder to stay on top."

THE HAMMER

Have you ever accidentally banged your thumb with a hammer? Imagine having that feeling *all over* your body! That's what it feels like to be nailed by San Francisco 49ers defensive back Ronnie Lott. Since coming to San Francisco in 1981, Lott has made the 49ers defense an aggressive, hard-hitting unit. World championships are won with bone-jarring play, and Ronnie Lott makes every hit count.

The cagey veteran inspires his teammates to play their best. Interceptions, fumbles and menacing stares are his trademarks. Opponents fear and respect his ability to go deep with a receiver or come up quickly and stick the ballcarrier.

Ronnie's presence on the field is enough to worry the other team. Four Super Bowl rings and seven trips to the Pro Bowl are pretty good reasons to stay away from Ronnie. Many times he has intercepted more than one pass in the same game.

Ronnie learned his trade at the University of Southern California. As a Trojan he was a star defensive back and earned All-America honors. He was the eighth player picked in the 1981 draft.

Ronnie is more than just a great player. His greatest talent may be his ability to bring out the best in the other 49er defenders. "I believe in

BENGAL ON THE PROWL

Three dislocated fingers would be enough to send most players to the locker room. Not Cincinnati's Tim Krumrie. He just snapped them back into place and didn't miss a play. His teammates call him "The Rabbit," because he gets so excited before games that he jumps up and down while waiting for the kickoff. His enthusiasm excites the Bengals defense.

Krumrie was a 10th-round draft pick in 1983, and at one time he was *sixth string!* But with hard work Krumrie earned a spot in the starting defense of the Bengals. He has also earned the respect of the NFL. "To stay on top, I have to do more than the other guy," he says. "It's like king of the mountain. Who can knock me off the top? If they work harder than me, they can come and try it."

weapon. Dan either leads or is among the leaders in four major offensive categories—passes thrown, completions, passing yardage and touchdown passes. In 1984 Marino threw for 5,084 yards—the best NFL single season ever. On October 23, 1988, he completed 35 of 60 passes for 521 yards and 3 touchdowns in one game! He passed for 4,000 or more yards 4 times in his first 6 seasons as a pro. He's also near the top in completion percentage and pass rating—among all-time quarterbacks and those still playing.

Not bad for a guy nobody wanted!

THE COMEBACK KID

There were 34 seconds to play in Super Bowl XXIII in Miami when San Francisco quarterback Joe Montana dropped to pass against Cincinnati. The 49ers were trailing, 16–13. Wide receiver John Taylor beat his man over the middle. Montana fired. Touchdown! The 49ers won the world champion-

playing from whistle to whistle," he says. "The football field is no place to stand around. Physical football wins games."

THE NFL's TOP GUN

Have you ever been playing football with your friends and you were the last one picked? Well, Dan Marino knows how that feels. In the 1982 draft 26 teams didn't want him. Dan was the next-to-last player chosen in the first round of the draft. Now many believe that Marino is the best passer ever to play football.

His pinpoint accuracy and arm strength provide the Dolphins with a terrific offensive

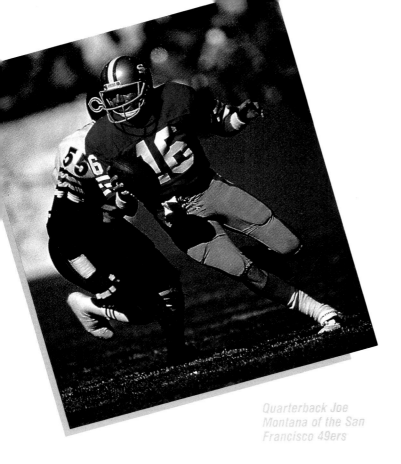

Quarterback Joe Montana of the San Francisco 49ers

ous back injury in 1986, which required surgery. He plays with just one thing in mind. "If you don't make each play work, there may not be another one," he says. "You have to play every snap like it's your last."

SIXTY-MINUTE RICE

San Francisco's Jerry Rice snaps, crackles and pops his way through an opposing pass defense. The most valuable player in Super Bowl XXIII, he has come a long way from tiny Mississippi Valley State where he played college football. Now Jerry dominates a game with his sure hands and running skill.

Blink and he's past you. Jerry leaves defensive backs wondering what happened. In Super Bowl XXIII he caught 11 passes for a record 215 yards. The NFL's Most Valuable Player in 1987, Jerry has a number of games with 100 or more receiving yards. He was named *Sports Illustrated* Player of the Year in 1986 and 1987. He has also played in four straight Pro Bowls.

Defensive backs give Jerry Rice plenty of room. But look out whenever Jerry catches a Joe Montana pass underneath the coverage. Rice is just as dangerous running with the football as he is catching it. With Jerry, any play can be a big play. He has the ability to make a routine catch something special.

An explosive player, Jerry creates scoring opportunities for the 49ers. A first-round draft choice in 1985, he has provided plenty of thrills in the city by the Bay.

GIANT POTENTIAL

Have you ever heard the word *potential*? It means that if you work hard at something, you might have what it takes to succeed. When the Giants drafted Phil Simms, he was the quarterback of tiny Morehead State. But the Giants thought he

ship, 20–16. It was the 49ers third Super Bowl victory in 8 years, and Montana passed for a Super Bowl record of 357 yards.

Such a performance is routine for Montana. For his entire career the 6′2″, 195-pound quarterback has been the "comeback kid." At Notre Dame he brought the Irish back from a 34–12 deficit to a 35–34 win over Houston in the 1977 Cotton Bowl.

He wasn't picked until the third round of the 1978 draft. But he earned a starting job by proving he could find a way to win. In the 1982 NFC championship game the 49ers trailed the Dallas Cowboys. With less than two minutes to play Joe drove San Francisco inside the Dallas 20. Time was running out when he dropped to pass one last time. At the last second Montana whipped the ball into the end zone where a diving receiver named Dwight Clark made the catch. Touchdown! That play put the 49ers in their first Super Bowl.

Joe Montana is the top-rated quarterback in NFL history. He has led San Francisco to four Super Bowl championships. Joe has been named the championship game's Most Valuable Player three times. Many, many times he has brought his team back when victory seemed out of reach. Perhaps his greatest comeback was from a seri-

Wide receiver Jerry Rice of the San Francisco 49ers

had the potential to be a great quarterback.

The Giants drafted Simms in the first round in 1979. He missed nearly all of the 1982 and 1983 seasons with horrible knee injuries. Most people thought he would quit football. But he didn't. He kept working. In 1984 Phil Simms realized his potential when he threw for 4,044 yards. Since then Simms has made his mark in the NFL. In 1986 he led his team to Super Bowl XXI with 12 straight victories. In the playoffs that year Simms was unbeatable. He threw four touchdown passes against San Francisco in the divisional playoff contest.

Then in one of the greatest Super Bowl performances ever, Phil completed a record 88 percent of his passes to beat the Denver Broncos. Phil threw 25 passes and completed 22 of them for 268 yards and 3 touchdowns. He was named the game's Most Valuable Player.

The 6′3″, 215-pound quarterback continues to lead by example. He always gives his best effort. A healthy Phil Simms makes the New York Giants a threat to any team in the league.

BAD NEWS BEAR

Where does a 6′, 228-pound Chicago Bear sleep? That's right—any place Mike Singletary wants. Middle linebackers are a different breed,

and Singletary may be the best all-around defensive player in the NFL.

Mike's teammates call him crazy. No wonder! Singletary's fierce tackling style broke the helmets of 16 opposing players during his college days at Baylor University. He has cracked four more in the NFL, including Eric Dickerson's in the NFC Championship in 1986. "It scares me when I think about it," he says. "I look around and I don't see anybody else breaking helmets. I hope there's nothing wrong with me."

At Baylor he earned All-America honors two years in a row. He was also named best player in the Southwest Conference twice. When the Bears picked Singletary in the second round of the 1981 draft they knew he was good. But nobody could have predicted that he would be named to six straight NFC Pro Bowl teams. In 1989 he was a unanimous pick as the best middle linebacker in the National Football Conference.

Singletary's teammates look to him for leadership. Since 1983 he's been the Bears defensive captain. Watch his eyes. They're on fire. He is constantly aware of who has the football and usually is the first to make the tackle.

Quarterback Phil Simms of the New York Giants

Linebacker Mike Singletary of the Chicago Bears

In one of his best games Mike roughed up the Dallas Cowboys with 16 tackles. On December 6, 1987, he cut his finger playing against the Minnesota Vikings. Doctors put 12 stitches in the finger, and Mike returned to lead a goal-line stand. The Bears won the game, 30–24, and wrapped up the NFC Central Division title.

"There are people who don't think I can keep playing like I have," Mike says. "But my critics don't have to play against me."

A KILLER GIANT

L awrence Taylor stands 6′3″. But he's head and shoulders above the rest of the NFL's outside linebackers. To go with it, he has got 243 pounds of solid muscle. "Lawrence Taylor, as he has for years, controls the game," says John Butler, a scout for

Linebacker Lawrence Taylor of the New York Giants

the Buffalo Bills. "He sets the standards for all the young linebackers coming out of college today."

Taylor has been to eight straight Pro Bowl games. How good is Taylor? Ask the Saints. Against New Orleans in 1988 LT sacked the quarterback 3 times, made 10 tackles and forced 2 fumbles.

Taylor was drafted by the Giants in the first round of the 1981 draft. His impact on the team was immediate. He received lots of attention at the University of North Carolina. But when he got to New York, he took the Meadowlands, where the Giants play, by storm.

Playing with speed and energy, LT forces other teams to run their plays away from him. He just starts switching sides. Trying to block Lawrence Taylor is like stepping in front of a moving car. "What's really amazing," says Bob Holloway, assistant general manager of the Minnesota Vikings, "is that every time we've played against him, he's *never* missed a tackle. Not one. You don't block Lawrence Taylor. You pray."

Find Lawrence Taylor and you will find the football. Whether it's in the hands of a quarterback, running back or receiver, when LT makes the hit the opponent hits the turf—hard. Compared to Lawrence Taylor, the rest of the league has trouble measuring up.

Running back Herschel Walker of the Minnesota Vikings

A Truck Named Herschel

W hen it comes to power and speed, Minnesota's Herschel Walker is simply the best. No other back in the NFL combines the size, strength and quickness of Walker. "I feel like if I want to get around you, I can run around you," Walker says. "And if I need to go over you, I can run over you. God has given me the talent to be a great back."

Herschel is a total player. He will lower his head for that extra yard up the middle. He will pick up speed as he turns the corner, winning the foot race to the goal line. He will catch a pass and turn the play into big yardage.

At the University of Georgia he won the 1982 Heisman Trophy. Three times he was named All-America with the highest number of votes possible. As a freshman he led the Bulldogs to the national championship. During his career he set 10 NCAA records.

Walker's ability was no secret when he signed with the New Jersey Generals of the United States Football League. In 3 seasons Herschel gained more than 7,000 yards and scored 61 touchdowns for the Generals. After the USFL folded he was signed by the Dallas Cowboys. Walker was the first player in NFL history to gain 700 yards both rushing and receiving in back-to-back years.

On November 15, 1987, he rushed for 173 yards against New England. His 60-yard score was the league's longest overtime touchdown run ever. It lifted the Dallas Cowboys to a 23–17 win over the Patriots.

Now the Herschel Walker show has moved north to Minnesota. Second to none in pure athletic ability, he's running toward greatness.

Defensive lineman Reggie White of the Philadelphia Eagles

THE MINISTER OF DEFENSE

A licensed Baptist preacher, Philadelphia defensive lineman Reggie White has earned the nickname "Minister of Defense." A 6′5″, 285-pound defensive end, he's a towering presence on the field. He has gained a reputation for aggressive, hard hitting and clean play.

"He's a great football player," says Eagles head coach Buddy Ryan. "I've been around great defensive linemen, and he's got to be the best, ability-wise, I've ever seen."

Three times in his career Reggie has had four sacks in the same game. He was the Most Valuable Player in the 1986 Pro Bowl. In just 12 games in 1987 he recorded the highest sack total of his career with 21. Since Reggie devours running backs at the line of scrimmage, most opponents run away from him. Many times he faces a double-team. Still, he uses his speed and strength to make the play.

"I've seen him put three-hundred-pounders on their butt a bunch of times. I get a kick out of that," says Philadelphia teammate Ron Heller. "No one guy can block him consistently....you just know you're in for a real long afternoon."

An All-America at the University of Tennessee, Reggie played two seasons with the Memphis Showboats of the United States Football League. The Eagles signed him when the USFL folded.

Reggie White is a leader on and off the field. "I want to lead this team to the Super Bowl," he says softly.

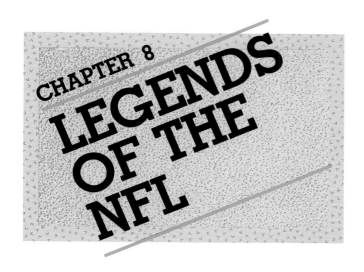

CHAPTER 8

LEGENDS OF THE NFL

THE NFL's OLDEST MAN

For 26 seasons George Blanda kicked and played quarterback in professional football. He played longer than anyone in the history of the game. He also scored a career record 2,002 points.

Blanda played for the Chicago Bears, Houston Oilers, Baltimore Colts and Oakland Raiders. In his playing days he kicked 335 field goals and 943 points after touchdown. He scored nine touchdowns, too.

Blanda graduated from the University of Kentucky. He began an 11-year career with the Chicago Bears in 1949. When the Bears released him in 1959 the ageless one's career looked over. But the new American Football League was just getting started, and the AFL teams wanted veterans. He signed with the Houston Oilers and in 1961 was named the league's most valuable player.

All things considered, Blanda's greatest season was with the Raiders in 1970. Against the Pittsburgh Steelers, Oakland starting quarterback Daryle Lamonica was lost with an injury. Blanda stepped into the job and threw for 3 touchdowns as the Raiders took a 31–14 win. Trailing Kansas City the next week, the Raiders called on Blanda for a game-tying field goal. The 48-yarder was right on the money.

When Lamonica was injured again later in the season, the 43-year-old Blanda came to the rescue in the middle of a game against Cleveland. He piloted the Raiders to a touchdown to tie the game. Then he kicked a game-winning 52-yard field goal. In the next two weeks Blanda rallied the Raiders to a come-from-behind win over the Denver Broncos and kicked a winning 16-yard field goal against the San Diego Chargers. Five times Blanda's skill saved the Raiders from defeat. The club won the AFC Western Division championship that year.

Blanda finally retired in 1975 at the age of 48, the oldest player in NFL history. Elected to the Pro Football Hall of Fame in 1981, he had played professionally in four decades. A tireless competitor, he is remembered for the longest career in professional football.

THE CAJUN CANNON

In 1969 the Pittsburgh Steelers were one of the NFL's oldest teams, having been in the league since its earliest days. But they had never won a championship. That year they were so bad that they only won one game. But they did one good thing that season: They drafted a quarterback named Terry Bradshaw.

Bradshaw was born in Shreveport, Louisiana. He was a terrific all-around athlete in high school and college at little Louisiana Tech. His greatest days, though, were with the Steelers.

Terry was named MVP in two Super Bowls, and he is one of only two quarterbacks in NFL history to lead his team to four Super Bowl championships. The other is Joe Montana.

In 1975, 1976, 1979 and 1980, the Steelers worked magic in the Super Bowl. Their defense, called the "steel curtain," kept the other team out of the end zone. Bradshaw and Pittsburgh's powerful offense dominated the other side of the line.

Terry threw long, spiral passes with pinpoint accuracy. More than that, he could run the football. He was at his best when the Steelers were down. With leadership and courage, Bradshaw inspired his teammates. One of his finest performances came in Super Bowl XIII when he threw for 318 yards and 4 touchdowns in a 35–31 win over the Dallas Cowboys.

Terry set Super Bowl records for lifetime yardage gained and most touchdown passes. His ability to read defenses and adjust according to his

Kicker/quarterback George Blanda

DIRT TOUGH

In nine NFL seasons Jim Brown was in a class by himself. From 1957 to 1965 he played for the Cleveland Browns and was the best running back in the league. Some still say he was the best ever.

Brown combined sheer power with great moves and incredible balance to rush for an NFL record 12,312 yards in his career. That mark stood for 19 seasons before Walter Payton overtook it in 1984. In 1963 Brown ran for 1,863 yards. That record lasted 10 years before it was broken by O. J. Simpson. Jim was also one of the most durable runners ever to play in the NFL. Through 122 football games he stayed almost injury-free.

It's important to remember that Brown set his career rushing record in seasons of 12 and 14 games. Later when Payton broke the record, the NFL season had been lengthened to 16 games. If Brown had played 16 games a year, one could only guess what he might have done.

Aside from his physical ability, Jim used his head. "I would say that I credit eighty percent of the success I had to the fact that I played a mental

Quarterback Terry Bradshaw

opponent's weakness set him apart from other quarterbacks. In his 13 seasons with the Pittsburgh Steelers, Terry helped transform the team from just another also-ran into a dynasty.

Since retirement Terry has acted in several movies. He also recorded a song, and his voice has become familiar on television as well. In 1989 he was inducted into the Pro Football Hall of Fame.

game," he recalls. "My game pivoted on having planned ahead of time every move I intended to make on the field. And I took pride in being dirt-tough."

One of Brown's best days ever came on November 1, 1959, when he rushed for 176 yards and 5 touchdowns against the NFL champion Baltimore Colts. Named the NFL's Rookie of the Year and Most Valuable Player in 1957, he was true to form that day. He capped off his last year in the NFL with his second MVP award.

When Brown retired in 1965 some thought he could still have played several more years. But Jim had reached the top and finished as the best in the game. He went on to a career in the movies and was elected to the NFL Hall of Fame in 1971.

MONSTER IN THE MIDDLE

Over the years the Chicago Bears have been known as the Monsters of the Midway. Dick Butkus, one of the best linebackers of all time, was Chicago's monster in the middle. He struck fear in the hearts of opposing ball carriers.

Butkus used his 245-pound body as a weapon. He was fast enough to catch a scrambling quarterback and powerful enough to make the big hit. A punishing tackler, he earned a reputation for intimidating opponents. Other players came to Chicago with a healthy respect, even a dread, of Dick Butkus.

Dick was an All-America at the University of Illinois. There was never any doubt in his mind which career was best suited for him. "There's only one thing I ever wanted to do," he says. "Play pro football. Everyone seems to be made for something. I've always felt that playing pro football was the thing I was supposed to do."

Butkus came to the Bears in 1965. He played eight seasons before badly injured knees forced him to retire. But even in that short career Dick made a name for himself in pro football. He was named to the Pro Bowl after all eight seasons.

When he signed a $200,000 contract with the Bears, Butkus was guaranteed more money than any defensive player in the NFL at the time. But he was worth it. He contributed in more ways than just making tackles. Because they recognized his ability, opponents altered their normal game plan when coming to Chicago.

Following his retirement, Dick pursued an acting and sports broadcasting career. Though his pro football days were relatively few, he left a lasting mark on the game. He was inducted into the Hall of Fame in 1979.

Running back Jim Brown

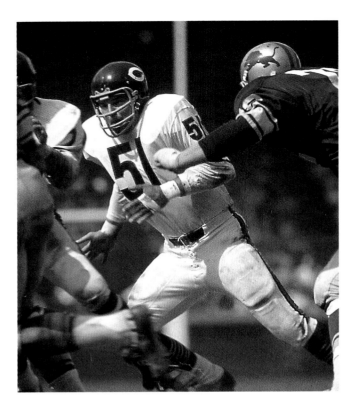

Linebacker Dick Butkus

In three straight seasons Zonk rushed for 1,000 yards or more. In two of three Super Bowls he rushed for more than 100 yards. He turned in his best performance with 33 carries for 145 yards and 2 touchdowns in Super Bowl VIII, and was named the game's Most Valuable Player.

One of the top power rushers ever in pro football, Larry played three seasons with the New York Giants. He spent one year with the Memphis Southmen of the World Football League. He was elected to Pro Football Hall of Fame in 1987.

THE QUIET LEADER

T alented, unselfish play-maker Bob Griese quarterbacked the Miami Dolphins during the team's glory days of the early 1970s. Bob's poise and intelligence made him a dangerous foe. He read

THE ZONK

A decade after the great Jim Brown was in his prime, another Syracuse University product began running over NFL defenses. Larry Csonka rushed his way into pro football history. His rock-solid effort every time out produced wins for the Miami Dolphins and aches and pains for competitors.

Csonka set the standard for powerful running backs in the mid-1970s. The Dolphins ran through the 1972 season unbeaten and won Super Bowl VII. In that year Larry Csonka tore opposing defenses apart. With fellow runners Jim Kiick and Mercury Morris and quarterback Bob Griese, Larry helped build Miami into one of the truly great teams in NFL history.

Known as "Zonk," Larry had a relentless, straight-ahead style of play. When it looked as if he was stopped, he lowered his head and churned his muscular legs to break tackles. Csonka had a special sense of where the first down marker and the end zone were. Trying to keep him behind either was a job few defenders could handle alone.

Running back
Larry Csonka

defenses like an open book. His grace under pressure meant many a win for Miami.

"He's probably the most unselfish guy I've ever been around," says Miami coach Don Shula. "He got as much of a thrill calling the right running play for a touchdown as he did connecting on a bomb. That's just his makeup." Bob Griese played team football, which earned him the respect of his team and the rest of the NFL.

Griese took the Dolphins to the Super Bowl three times and brought back two world championships. The Dolphins won almost 70% of the games in which he played. In 1980, his last season, Bob joined pro football's quarterback elite with more than 25,000 career passing yards. During the same game that he reached that career passing goal, Bob suffered a shoulder injury that forced his retirement.

Seven times in his career Bob Griese threw for 2,000 or more yards in a single season. He leads the Dolphins in Pro Bowl appearances with six. With apparent ease he could connect with wide receivers Paul Warfield and Nat Moore on fly patterns. He was effective throwing to running back Jim Kiick out of the backfield. And of course he called on Larry Csonka for power running. The great thing about Griese was that he instinctively knew which weapon to use.

Miami owner Joe Robbie once called Bob Griese "the cornerstone of the franchise." In their greatness, the Dolphins relied on the savvy of the Purdue graduate. And he never disappointed them.

THE MIRACLE CATCH

The year was 1972. The Steelers were losing a playoff game to the Oakland Raiders, 7–6, in the closing seconds of the contest. Quarterback Terry Bradshaw threw a desperate pass against the vaunted Raider defense.

The ball flew 40 yards downfield. A Steeler and a Raider collided trying to catch it. The ball spun crazily into the air. Just before it hit the turf, a running back named Franco Harris pulled it off his shoe tops and raced 42 yards for the game-winning touchdown.

Quarterback Bob Griese

Known as the "Immaculate Reception," that play alone was enough to keep the name Franco Harris alive forever among football fans. But Franco did more—much more. His career began slowly, but when Franco caught fire he blazed a trail to the Super Bowl.

With Franco running the football as only he could, the Steelers won four NFL championships. In Super Bowl IX he rushed for a record 158 yards and earned the game's MVP award. Seven times in his career, he rushed for over 1,000 yards in a season. In 13 NFL years he rushed for 12,120 yards.

At Penn State University Harris played in the shadow of Lydell Mitchell. In the pros, however, he stepped into the spotlight. When he retired in 1984 he was the only AFC player ever to appear in eight straight Pro Bowls. His record in playoff competition speaks for itself—1,482 rushing yards.

"Franco was the key man on our ball club," says former Steeler Joe Greene. "All we needed was the catalyst and Franco was it. He could have come here four years earlier and not made any difference at all, but that year [Super Bowl IX], he was just what we needed."

Franco gave the Steelers everything he had and opponents much more than they wanted. His

Running back Franco Harris in Superbowl IX.

gutsy, never-say-die play kept the Steelers riding high. Harris will be remembered as the bruising power runner who led the Steelers to greatness.

More to Life than Football

Seattle Seahawks wide receiver Steve Largent knows how it feels to be too little and too slow to play football. After his college football career the 5′ 11″, 190-pound Largent signed with the Houston Oilers. The Oilers told him he wasn't good enough and cut him. So he tried out with the Seattle Seahawks. He worked very hard and studied his plays.

Today, 14 years later, Steve Largent is the greatest wide receiver in NFL history. He has more than 800 catches for more than 12,700 yards. Steve makes up for his lack of speed with grit, smarts and desire.

Steve is also tough. In 1988 Largent suffered a concussion the first week of the season, an eye injury two weeks later and injuries to his foot and thumb the next week. He missed only one game that season. Steve never complains about pain or injuries. "I've learned to be thankful," Largent says. "There is more to life than just football. I found that out a few years ago."

On November 11, 1985, Steve's wife, Terry, gave birth to their fourth child, Kramer James Largent, who was born with spina bifida—an

Wide receiver Steve Largent

exposed spinal cord. Doctors told him his baby could end up retarded.

"I couldn't believe it," Largent recalls. "I huddled in a corner of the delivery room and cried bitterly for my son. It was a situation that was even more difficult for me, an athlete, whose livelihood depends on agility, to comprehend."

Today, four years and several operations later, Kramer has near-perfect health.

"Kramer has been a lesson to our whole family, and especially me, a jock, who all these years has been fighting to succeed," Largent says. "If you can confront what life deals you, you will grow as a person. I don't know yet what I'll do after football. Sure, I'm scared. But Kramer has it harder that I ever will. It won't be easy. But Kramer and I, with God's help, will do all right."

"I GUARANTEE IT..."

Brash and bold, Joe Willie Namath created a sensation when he signed with the New York Jets of the old American Football League. The Jets made Namath the highest-paid rookie in football history. He didn't disappoint them.

Joe brought more than just ability to professional football. He also brought charisma. Before the merger of the NFL and AFL, Namath attracted attention for the new AFL on and off the field.

In 1968 Joe Willie led the Jets to the AFL championship and a date in Super Bowl III with the powerful Baltimore Colts of the NFL. The Colts were favored to win the game by at least 18 points. Nobody gave the Jets a chance. Nobody, that is, except Joe Namath.

"We're going to beat the Colts on Sunday," he roared. "I guarantee it." People thought he was crazy. But then his Jets went out and controlled the game from start to finish. They won, 16–7, and Joe Namath was a hero.

Super Bowl III was the greatest day of the greatest season in the career of Joe Namath. He completed 17 of 28 passes in the victory and was named the game's Most Valuable Player. Joe, however, never regained the greatness of that season. A number of serious knee injuries, a broken wrist and a shoulder separation cut short his career.

Still, his tight, spiral passes were beauties. They earned him a reputation as a great passer. Twice he threw for more than 400 yards in a single game. He kept his cool under pressure and performed.

"Broadway Joe" excited fans on and off the football field. Slowed by his injuries, Joe Namath

Quarterback Joe Namath

Defensive tackle Merlin Olsen as he dumped New Orleans Saints quarterback Archie Manning for a loss

had a brief rise to the top in pro football. He will always be remembered for predicting the win in Super Bowl III and then playing the game of his life to make it come true. Joe Willie entered the Hall of Fame in 1985.

THE LEADER OF THE FEARSOME FOURSOME

Merlin Olsen played blue-collar football. He was a quiet man, but his play at defensive tackle spoke loudly. Olsen was the backbone of one of the best defensive lines ever in the NFL—the famed "Fearsome Foursome" of the Los Angeles Rams in the late 1960s and early 1970s.

Olsen played 15 seasons in the NFL. He was selected to the Pro Bowl an amazing 14 times. He accomplished all this lined up across the ball from the best offensive linemen the other team had. He was constantly double-teamed (covered by two players).

Always an intelligent player, Olsen realized that strength alone would not make a football player great. "A good defensive lineman has to be part charging buffalo and part ballet dancer," Olsen says. "And he has to know when to be which. It's more an emotional state and ability to concentrate. If you haven't got those, you can't generate the horsepower to make the right thing happen."

Olsen became the leader of the "Fearsome Foursome," which included Deacon Jones, Rosey Grier and Lamar Lundy. Together this group of the toughest linemen in football had the ability to completely dominate a game. Olsen and company were respected and feared throughout the National Football League.

"We never had a bad game from Merlin Olsen," says ex-Rams coach George Allen, "and more often than not you got a great one."

In a game in 1967 with Green Bay, the Rams trailed with little time left. The "Fearsome Foursome" stopped the Packers on three straight plays. Olsen blocked the punt on fourth down. The Rams took the ball at the Green Bay five-yard line and scored the winning touchdown on the next play. In a divisional playoff against Baltimore the following week, Olsen and his teammates sacked Johnny Unitas seven times and caused a pair of interceptions in a 34–10 win.

Olsen was inducted into the Hall of Fame in 1982. After retirement, he hardly slowed down at all. Merlin has become a successful sports broadcaster, has appeared on NBC's "Little House on the Prairie" and has starred in two series of his own, "Father Murphy" and "Aaron's Way."

SWEETNESS

Watching Walter Payton run made it easy to understand why his teammates nicknamed him "Sweetness." It is also easy to understand why Sweetness left a bitter taste with all the

Running back
Walter Payton

opponents who tried—unsuccessfully—to slow him down during his long career with the Chicago Bears.

Payton burst onto the NFL stage in 1975 as a rookie from tiny Jackson State University in Mississippi. His rookie statistics weren't that impressive, but after that first season things started to happen. The combination of hard-nosed, gritty football and smooth, effortless running came together in Payton as it had in few players ever before.

In 13 seasons Walter rushed for over 1,000 yards 10 times. He made it to the Pro Bowl nine times. He led the Bears to a 15–1 season and the world championship in Super Bowl XX. But his greatest achievement by far was breaking Jim Brown's career rushing record with 16,726 yards.

"He has the ability to come up with the big play each week," said a teammate. "He does things nobody else can do." Payton brought to pro football an incredible combination of strength, endurance and speed. Once he broke through the line or turned the corner, he was harder to catch than anyone in the NFL.

Walter's best day was November 20, 1977. Shaking off the effects of the flu as easily as he did Viking defenders, Payton ran wild. On 40 carries against Minnesota he gained 275 yards to break O. J. Simpson's single-game rushing record.

At the end of the 1987 season Payton called an end to his unbelievable career. He held 10 NFL records including rushing touchdowns, games over 100 yards, consecutive seasons as the league's leading rusher, rushing attempts and consecutive 1,000-yard seasons. By just about anybody's standards, Walter Payton was the best running back in pro-football history.

BORN TO RUN

Bruce Springsteen once wrote a song called "Born to Run." That song would have summed up the career of Gayle Sayers, a legendary Chicago Bears running back who once claimed that he too was born to run. Whenever Sayers got the ball his speed kicked up the breeze in the Windy City, as Chicago is often called.

Elected to the Hall of Fame in 1977, Sayers was another fantastic player whose career was cut short by injuries. Both his knees were seriously

Running back Gale Sayers

"I just looked for the hole and let instinct get me loose," Sayers says. That was the key to his greatness. Running the football was instinctive to him. If he had not been injured Gayle Sayers would probably have completely rewritten football history.

THE JUICE

The Heisman Trophy is awarded to the best player in college football. None of its winners was more deserving than Orenthal James Simpson of the University of Southern California. O. J., also known as "the Juice," ran with such a graceful, fluid motion in the open field that he was compared with Gayle Sayers.

For the onrushing defender the Juice came and went in a flash. His lightning speed and tremendous balance made him a threat every time he touched the football. "I didn't feel I had to challenge tacklers," he says. "I ran a lot by instinct and how much I could see when I'm through the hole."

Drafted by the lowly Buffalo Bills in 1969, Simpson suffered through three average seasons without a strong offensive line. When Lou Saban came to Buffalo as head coach in 1972, Buffalo's strategy changed. Offensively, O. J. would be the key to any success the team might have.

Shaking off the disappointments of the previous years Simpson rushed for 1,251 yards that season. In 1973 he began a quest to become the first back in the NFL to rush for 2,000 in one season.

In the final game of the year against the New York Jets, O. J. broke Jim Brown's single season rushing mark of 1,863 yards. He finished the year with 2,003 yards. Eric Dickerson bettered O. J.'s record in 1984 running 2,105 yards in 16 games.

Not only was O. J. a great athlete he was a class act off the field. When reporters crowded the locker room after his record-breaking day, O. J. praised each member of his offensive line, saying, "I want to introduce the cats who've done the job for me all year."

The Juice had other great days. In one game he rushed for 273 yards in a game against the Detroit Lions. He finished his career at home in

hurt ending a spectacular, though brief, stint in the NFL. Sayers' raw talent—a combination of speed, agility and elegance—left players, fans and coaches speechless.

After leaving the University of Kansas he gave the Bears an incredible rookie year. On December 12, 1965, he scored *six* touchdowns in one game against the San Francisco 49ers. Only two other players, Ernie Nevers and Dub Jones, had done it before. Three of Sayers' touchdown runs covered 85, 80 and 50 yards.

"Congratulations on the greatest one-man performance I've ever witnessed on a football field," a startled Nevers said to the young superstar. "Your brilliance will long be remembered in this sport."

In six short seasons Sayers provided some unforgettable moments. In 1969 he returned from a knee injury to lead the NFL in rushing. He returned a record six kickoffs for touchdowns in his career. He was selected to the Pro Bowl five times and named MVP in three of those games.

Running back O.J. Simpson after setting another NFL record.

When Dallas had the lead late in the game, the Packers faced the cold, the clock and the Cowboy defenders.

Starr huddled his troops. He then set to work marching them down the field. The Packers reached the Dallas 1-yard line on third down with only 16 seconds left in the game. It was do or die for the Pack. Starr sliced through the line just far enough for the winning touchdown. It was one of the greatest finishes ever. Bart Starr and the Packers had gutted it out.

In Super Bowl I, Bart completed 16 of 23 passes for 250 yards and 2 touchdowns to lead the Pack to victory. He threw a 62-yard touchdown pass to Boyd Dowler in Super Bowl II and finished with 202 yards on 13 of 24 passes. Starr threw a record 294 passes without an interception in the 1964 and 1965 seasons. He retired from football in 1971 but returned to the Packers as coach from 1974 through 1983. In 1977 he became a member of the Hall of Fame.

San Francisco with the 49ers and was elected to the Hall of Fame in 1985. O. J. Simpson recognized and made the most of his own ability.

THE LEADER OF THE PACK

The Green Bay Packers of the 1960s were one of the NFL's great dynasties. Bart Starr, a seventeenth-round draft pick, was their leader. Starr was one of the most accurate passers in NFL history, and the Most Valuable Player in Super Bowls I and II. In the pre–Super Bowl days, he guided the Packers to NFL championships in 1961, 1962, 1965, 1966 and 1967. Bart was a quiet and reserved player. Yet his will to win brought victories to Green Bay.

In one of the most memorable football games ever played the Packers met the Dallas Cowboys in the 1967 NFC championship game. With minus-13 degree temperatures, the game went down in history as the "Ice Bowl." The Cowboys "Doomsday Defense" was the best in the league.

Quarterback Bart Starr

Quarterback Roger Staubach

ROGER THE DODGER

Former Dallas quarterback Roger Staubach was a master scrambler. He ducked blitzing linebackers and side-stepped tacklers with ease. Nicknamed "Artful Dodger," Staubach was resourceful. Time after time he brought the Dallas Cowboys from the edge of defeat to victory.

During 10 years with Dallas, Roger quarterbacked the Cowboys to six NFC championship games, four Super Bowls and two world championships. He was a five-time Pro Bowl selection. The Cowboys lost a close game to the Colts in Super Bowl V. But the next year Staubach became the starting quarterback, and the Cowboys rolled to a 24–3 win over the Miami Dolphins in Super Bowl VI. The "Artful Dodger" was the game's Most Valuable Player.

Staubach was probably the best quarterback ever when the game was on the line. He led the Cowboys to 23 come-from-behind wins. On 14 occasions he pulled Dallas through in the last 2 minutes of the game or in overtime.

Roger will probably be remembered most for a single play. The Cowboys trailed the Minnesota Vikings late in a 1975 playoff game. With less than a minute to play, the situation looked hopeless. Staubach dropped back from the 50-yard line and made a desperate pass to an area flooded with defensive backs. Wide receiver Drew Pearson pinned the ball against his hip. He fell backward into the end zone. The officials signaled a touchdown, and Dallas had a miracle victory. The play will always be known as "Hail Mary." It was one of pro football's greatest moments.

Staubach graduated from the U.S. Naval Academy where he won the Heisman Trophy. Dallas drafted him in 1964, but Roger had to spend four years in the navy before he ever took a snap for the Cowboys. "He was the best quarterback to come out of college in years," says Tex Schramm, who was then president of the Cowboys. "He was well worth waiting for."

Roger Staubach's poise and confidence made winners of the Dallas Cowboys. He found an opportunity to win and made the most of it. Roger was inducted into the Hall of Fame in 1985.

THE MAN WITH THE GOLDEN ARM

He has been called "the Man with the Golden Arm," but most people simply called him "Johnny U." When Johnny Unitas left pro football his name was synonomous with winning. He had passed for an amazing 40,239 yards and 290 touchdowns. He also led the NFL in pass attempts and completions.

Unitas spent 18 seasons in the NFL. During the time he played quarterback for the Baltimore Colts, his team won two NFL championships. When it came to playing under pressure, Unitas was the best. "He's got ice water in his veins," a teammate said.

In the NFL's first sudden-death overtime game, Unitas delivered. With the score tied 17–17, Johnny calmly took the Colts 80 yards in 12 plays. From the one-yard line, running back Alan Ameche scored the winning touchdown against the New York Giants. The Colts were the 1958 NFL champions. Some still remember that game as the greatest ever played.

For all his greatness Johnny Unitas almost didn't get a chance to play pro football. He wanted

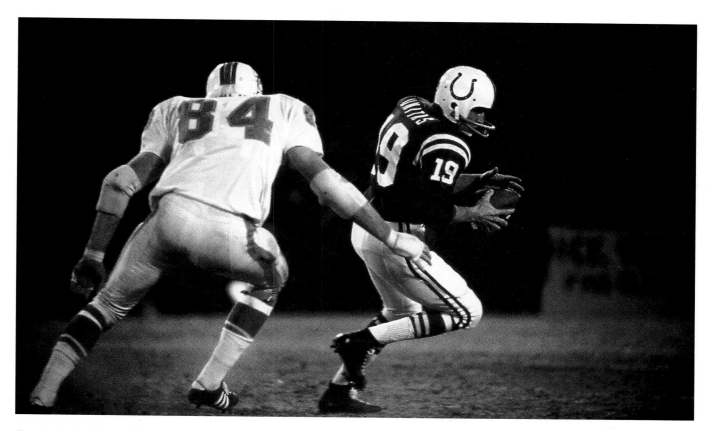

Quarterback Johnny Unitas

to go to Notre Dame, but the Irish turned him down because of his size. So he went to the University of Louisville instead.

Unitas was drafted in the ninth round but got cut. He went to work for a construction company and played semi-pro ball for $6 a game. Then his chance came when the Colts called him after their starting quarterback got hurt.

Johnny made the most of his opportunity. Under his guidance, the Colts won 47 straight games over four seasons from 1956 to 1960. In each of those games, Unitas threw a touchdown pass.

Named to the Pro Football Hall of Fame in 1979, Unitas never gave up. He held on to his dream. And that dream, through hard work, became reality.

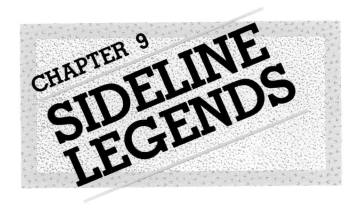

CHAPTER 9
SIDELINE LEGENDS

MR. COMMISSIONER

Promoter, negotiator, peacemaker and judge Alvin "Pete" Rozelle held the post of NFL Commissioner for 29 years. During that time the National Football League entered its modern age. Rozelle led the league during a period of growth, transition and change.

NFL Commissioner Bert Bell died suddenly in 1959. The following year a power struggle took place in the league. Who would be the new commissioner? The old and the new battled for control. The voting was dead-even. Then someone suggested Pete Rozelle.

Since 1957 Rozelle had been general manager of the Los Angeles Rams. He was young. He was energetic. He was elected commissioner on the twenty-third vote.

Pete went to work right away. He negotiated television contracts for the league. This gave the NFL the money to pay its bills. He also dealt with the problems caused by the rival American Football League. Later the World Football League and the United States Football League unsuccessfully challenged the NFL.

During Pete's years as commissioner he was forced to make many tough decisions. Part of a commissioner's job is to make sure players follow certain rules on and off the field. If players didn't follow those rules, it was Pete Rozelle who decided what their punishment should be.

Rozelle also led the NFL through its successful merger with the American Football League. When the two leagues agreed to become one, it was a good decision for the players, coaches and fans. The NFL's popularity grew.

As commissioner he held the NFL together through two players' strikes. Rozelle has also dealt with issues like drug abuse. As the times have changed, the commissioner and the NFL have changed as well. Under Rozelle new teams have come into the NFL. The competition has been tough every year.

There were setbacks and problems during Pete Rozelle's years as commissioner. He met those challenges head-on. Rozelle accepted responsibility. He made decisions based on what was best for football rather than what might serve a single person or team.

Along the way Rozelle was not always liked by everyone in football. He and some of the team owners disagreed from time to time. But every time an issue arose Pete Rozelle tried to do the right thing. His leadership brought pro football a new time of prosperity. When Pete Rozelle retired in 1989, an era ended.

Commissioner Pete Rozelle presiding over the 1967 NFL draft.

BUBBLE GUM BEAR

Nobody hates losing more than Mike Ditka of the Chicago Bears. On December 14, 1987, the San Francisco 49ers beat the Chicago Bears 41–0. It was a terrible night for the Bears. The 49ers fans were laughing at Ditka as he left the field. He was so angry that he took a big wad of bubble gum out of his mouth and threw it at a fan. Bull's-eye! It hit the fan right between the eyes.

"Iron Mike" learned football from two of the game's best coaches—the Bears' George Halas and Tom Landry of the Cowboys. When he took over in Chicago in the middle of the 1982 season, the Bears were loaded with problems. They won only three of the nine games Ditka coached that year. The next year they finished an even 8–8. Then the Bears started a string of playoff appearances. Their best year came in 1985. Ditka's team finished the regular season with a 15–1 record. Then they overwhelmed the New England Patriots in Super Bowl XX, 46–10.

From 1985 to 1988, the Bears won 52 games. That's more than any other NFL team has ever won. Ditka's will to win rubs off on his players and

Head coach Mike Ditka of the Chicago Bears

assistant coaches. He is very intense. But Ditka understands the pressure of football because he played it. He was a star tight end for the Bears, the Eagles and the Cowboys, and NFL Rookie of the Year in 1961. He played in five Pro Bowls. Ditka caught 75 passes in 1964, a record for tight ends. He was named to the Hall of Fame in 1988.

Mike Ditka surrounds himself with winners. "Winning isn't everything," he said once. "But it beats the heck out of losing." Once after the Bears lost a game, Ditka got so angry that he punched a locker as hard as he could and broke his hand. "You can never be perfect in football," Ditka says. "But perfection is what we strive for. If we constantly strive to get better, we *will* improve our football team."

HAIL TO THE CHIEF

Joe Gibbs is the chief of the Washington Redskins. Even though Gibbs never played a down in pro football, he has earned the respect of the entire NFL. The reason? *He wins.* Twice he has won the Super Bowl, which prompted *Sport* magazine to call him the best coach in the NFL.

In his first eight years as Redskins coach Joe's teams won four NFC Eastern Division crowns and four NFC championships. The year before he took over, the Redskins lost 10 games. But under Gibbs, they turned things around.

In the strike-shortened 1982 season, Gibbs put together a winning combination. The passing and scrambling of quarterback Joe Theismann teamed with the running of powerful John Riggins. That year the Redskins defeated the Miami Dolphins 27–17 to win Super Bowl XVII. They went back the next year but lost to the Los Angeles Raiders.

In 1988 Gibbs and the Redskins won Super Bowl XXII, ripping the Denver Broncos 42–10. Writers and coaches called the Washington leader a genius. He is one of the winningest active coaches in the NFL.

Gibbs likes to keep his offense balanced. He mixes the run and the pass. That combination is a big reason for the Redskins success. Since Joe Gibbs came to Washington, only the San Francisco 49ers have won more games.

Head coach Joe Gibbs of the Washington Redskins

Gibbs learned patience and discipline while playing guard, tight end and linebacker for San Diego State. He coached at the college level for nine seasons before serving as the St. Louis Cardinals offensive backfield coach from 1973 through 1977. In 1978 he became Tampa Bay's offensive coordinator and then moved to San Diego and served in the same position for two seasons. While Gibbs was with the Chargers they won the AFC West title once and led the NFL in passing both years. Today Joe Gibbs is still patient and hard-working. He spends many nights working until two or three A.M. Sometimes he spends the night on his office sofa. "If you want to be the best in this business," Gibbs says, "you have to work for it."

FROM WORST TO FIRST

In the three seasons before Chuck Noll took over as head coach, the Pittsburgh Steelers had won only 11 games in three years. In Chuck's first season they were even worse,

slipping to 1–13. But Noll patiently began building Pittsburgh into one of the best teams ever in the NFL. He drafted the right players. He built a defense called the "steel curtain." In 1972 his team won 11 of 14 games and won their division for the first time in history.

Today Noll is one of only four coaches in NFL history who has stayed with the same team 21 years or longer—he started with the Steelers in 1969. Noll built the team by drafting players like "Mean" Joe Greene, Lynn Swann and Terry Bradshaw. Under Noll's leadership, the Steelers made pro-football history. Before the San Francisco 49ers won Super Bowl XXIV in 1990, Pittsburgh was the only NFL team to win four Super Bowls. They took the prize in 1975, 1976, 1979 and 1980. Because of their dominance during that time, the Steelers are often referred to as the "Team of the Seventies."

Chuck Noll has spent nearly 40 years in football as a player and a coach. After a college career at the University of Dayton, Chuck played seven seasons with the Cleveland Browns. He was a teammate of the great Jim Brown at Cleveland. The Browns won two NFL championships while Chuck was a player.

In 1960 Chuck took his first coaching job with the Los Angeles Chargers. The Chargers later moved to San Diego. While Noll was in Los Angeles, the Chargers won the championship of the AFL. Noll also worked with another coaching great, Don Shula of the Miami Dolphins, when they were both members of the Baltimore Colts staff. In Chuck's three years as a Baltimore assistant the Colts lost only seven games. They made it all the way to the Super Bowl in 1969 but they lost to the New York Jets.

The next season Noll took over the Steelers where he took a last-place team from worst to first.

THE WINNING EDGE

Miami's Don Shula's name is synonymous with winning. "I'm just a guy who rolls up his sleeves and goes to work," he says. "I don't have peace of mind until I know I've given the game everything

Head coach Chuck Noll of the Pittsburgh Steelers (left) and his Miami Dolphins counterpart, Don Shula.

I can. The whole idea is to somehow get an edge. Sometimes it takes just a little extra something to get that edge but you have to have a winning edge."

Somehow Shula has always found that edge. He was a running back at tiny John Carroll University but played hard enough that he got noticed and was drafted by the Cleveland Browns in 1951. He played four seasons with the Colts and one with the Redskins before going into coaching.

After coaching at Virginia and Kentucky he broke into the NFL as an assistant coach with the Detroit Lions. In 1963 he was named head coach at Baltimore. The Colts had played only average football the three years before he arrived but Shula made them NFL champions. When he went to Miami in 1970, the Dolphins had been perennial losers. Shula combined his knowledge of football with the talents of players like Larry

Csonka and Bob Griese, and by 1972 his Miami Dolphins might have been the best team ever to play in the NFL. In their first Super Bowl season, the Dolphins finished with an undefeated 17–0 record. The next year the Dolphins lost only two games before winning another NFL championship against the Minnesota Vikings. Since then Shula has been to the Super Bowl three more times.

Shula has won more football games than any other active coach in the NFL. On the all-time list, only George Halas of the Chicago Bears won more. Shula was the youngest coach to win 100 games and the youngest to win 200 games. He also coached the Baltimore Colts in Super Bowl III when they lost to the New York Jets.

"If I'm remembered for anything as a coach," he says, "I hope it's for playing within the rules. I also hope it will be said that my teams showed class and dignity in victory and defeat."

SECTION IV:

INSIDE THE NFL

CHAPTER 10
THE AFC

EASTERN DIVISION

Buffalo Bills
Indianapolis Colts
Miami Dolphins
New England Patriots
New York Jets

BUFFALO STANCE

I t hasn't been easy to be a fan of the Buffalo Bills. Some years, the Bills have won championships. In other years, they've been lucky to win a game.

The Bills got their start in 1959 as a member of the AFL. Ralph Wilson, who was an owner of the Detroit Lions, organized the team and named it the Bills after Buffalo Bill Cody, a famous pioneer of the American West. In 1964 the Bills won their first championship when they defeated the San Diego Chargers in the old American Football League. They repeated as the best in the AFL the next year and won their division in 1966. But it took 14 years for a Buffalo team to win another title.

Through the years, the Bills have had two great running backs. Cookie Gilchrist was the

first in the AFL to rush for 1,000 or more yards, which he did in 1962 when he gained 1,096 yards. The other was O. J. Simpson, who became a legend as one of the finest running backs ever in football. Simpson, better known as "The Juice," set many records with the Bills, with whom he played from 1969 to 1978. He also kept the fans interested in a team that wasn't winning many games. During Simpson's best years, Buffalo fans taunted the rival Miami Dolphins, saying, "Miami's got the oranges but Buffalo's got the Juice."

The Bills have played their home games at Rich Stadium since 1973. Head coach Marv Levy joined the team in 1986. They reached the AFC championship game in 1988 but lost to the Cincinnati Bengals. That year they won the AFC Eastern Division championship, their first since 1980. Levy has the team headed in the right direction and today, with players like quarterback Jim Kelly and linebacker Cornelius Bennett, the Bills and their fans are looking for a Super Bowl.

Rain or shine, running back O.J. Simpson of the Buffalo Bills was always ahead of the pack.

This field goal by Jim O'Brien gave the Baltimore Colts a 16-13 win over Dallas in Super Bowl V.

TIME LINE

1969—The Bills sign O. J. Simpson to a long-term contract after tough negotiations.

1973—Simpson finishes the season with a record 2,003 yards beating Jim Brown's old mark.

1978—O. J. Simpson is traded to the San Francisco 49ers.

1980—The Bills win their first division championship in 14 long years.

1988—The Bills win their division title but lose the AFC championship game to Cincinnati.

INDIANA HOOSIERS

On March 29, 1984, the moving vans pulled out of Baltimore, Maryland in the middle of the night. They carried the NFL's Colts to their new home in Indianapolis, closing the book on more than 30 seasons in Baltimore. Owner Robert Irsay moved the team because he felt the city of Baltimore wasn't fair to his team.

Baltimore almost didn't have a team to move. In 1950 the original Colts went broke. The Dallas Texans moved to Baltimore in 1952 and became the new Colts.

During their years in Baltimore, the Colts had their ups and downs. With legendary Johnny Unitas as quarterback and running backs like Alan Ameche and Tom Matte, the Colts made history. They won NFL championships in 1958, 1959 and 1968. They lost Super Bowl III to the New York Jets in 1969 but in 1971 the Colts won Super Bowl V with a 16–13 win over the Dallas Cowboys.

Since then the Colts have won AFC East titles in 1972, 1975, 1976, 1977 and 1987. There have been several losing seasons and coaching changes. They have yet to match the success of the Unitas era.

Coach Ron Meyer, with the Colts since 1986, hopes his team can find that combination of skill and luck which winners need. Eric Dickerson, the leading active rusher in the NFL, is one big reason for Meyer's optimism. The Colts traded several high draft picks for Dickerson. Eric holds the league record for yardage gained in a single season with 2,105. Quarterback Jack Trudeau is also a key player.

When the Colts left Baltimore their long-time fans were crushed. But the people of Indianapolis welcomed them enthusiastically. The team's home is now the big, modern Hoosier Dome. With some luck Meyer and his players hope to give Indianapolis the kind of team that made the Colts famous in Baltimore.

TIME LINE

1958—In possibly the greatest game ever played, the Colts defeat the New York Giants for the NFL championship, 23–17.

1972—Robert Irsay becomes majority owner of the Colts.

1973—Johnny Unitas is traded to the San Diego Chargers.

1984—The Colts move to Indianapolis.

1986—Ron Meyer is named the team's 12th head coach.

SMART AS A DOLPHIN?

Every NFL team dreams of a perfect season. In 1973 the Miami Dolphins did more than dream—they *had* a perfect season. Coach Don Shula put together one of the greatest teams in NFL history. The Dolphins rolled through the rest of the league and finished the season as Super Bowl champions with a 17–0 record.

The Dolphins began their climb to the top of the NFL in 1965. Joe Robbie, an attorney from Philadelphia, teamed with actor Danny Thomas to buy the team. Mrs. Robert Swanson won a contest to name the new team. She suggested "Dolphins" because dolphins are smart. They're also commonly found in the ocean off Miami.

The Miami Dolphins took their lumps early. Then in 1970 Shula was named head coach. He got the team started on the road to fame. The following season, they made the playoffs for the first time.

Just two seasons after taking the Miami job Shula had the Dolphins in the Super Bowl. They lost 24–3 to the Dallas Cowboys but they learned

valuable lessons. The next time things would be different.

The dream season followed. The Dolphins defeated the Washington Redskins 14–7 in Super Bowl VII. Quarterback Bob Griese was the team leader. Running backs Larry Csonka, Jim Kiick and Eugene "Mercury" Morris were key offensive players along with receivers Paul Warfield and Nat Moore. Lineman Manny Fernandez, linebacker Nick Buoniconti and safeties Dick Anderson and Jake Scott were the best of what was called the "No Name" defense. (Linebacker Bob Matheson coined the name when he told a reporter, "There are no big names or superstars on this defense. We're just a bunch of no-names.") Most football fans say they've never seen another NFL team with as much talent as that Miami team.

The Dolphins stayed on top one more year. In 1974 they beat the Minnesota Vikings 24–7 in Super Bowl VIII. After the season Csonka, Kiick and Warfield left the Dolphins.

Since their glory days the Dolphins have had other talented teams. They've been back to the Super Bowl twice in the 1980s but lost both games—in 1983 they were beaten by the Redskins and in 1985 they lost to the 49ers.

Shula's Super Bowl teams in the past 10 years were not as talented as his previous championship teams but he has put together a group of fine young athletes. Record-setting quarterback Dan Marino is an incredible passer. Receivers Mark Clayton and Mark Duper are his favorite targets. Linebackers Hugh Green and John Offerdahl set the defensive pace. When Don Shula first came to Miami, he told his players winning took hard work. Today he's the most successful active coach in the NFL.

TIME LINE

1970—Don Shula becomes head coach of the Dolphins.

1973—Miami caps a perfect 17–0 season with a 14–7 win over Washington in Super Bowl VII.

1974—Miami beats the Vikings 24–7 in Super Bowl VIII.

1980—Quarterback Bob Griese retires.

1983—Washington gets revenge by beating Miami 27–17 in Super Bowl XVII.

Miami running back Jim Kiick in a place he knew well—the end zone.

1984—Dan Marino becomes the first NFL quarterback to pass for more than 5,000 yards.

1985—After a record-setting season by quarterback Dan Marino, Miami gets shut down by the 49ers, 38–16, in the Super Bowl.

THE PRIDE OF FOXBORO

The New England Patriots began in Boston in 1959. They were the eighth team in the AFL. Billy Sullivan, Jr., was their founder. In 1970 the Patriots moved to Sullivan Stadium in Foxboro, Massachusetts, outside of Boston and officially changed their name from the Boston Patriots to the New England Patriots.

Over the years winning hasn't been easy for the Patriots. They won the AFL Eastern Division in 1963 but it wasn't until 1976 that they reached the playoffs in the NFL. They didn't win their division until 1978.

Coach Ron Meyer guided the Pats into the playoffs in 1983 when they lost once again. But in 1984 former NFL star Raymond Berry became the team's head coach. He was determined to take the Patriots to the Super Bowl. They made it the next year but the tough Chicago Bears pounded the Patriots, 46–10, in Super Bowl XX.

Berry, a Hall of Fame receiver, has battled many problems in New England as he works on resurrecting the Patriots. The team overcame the drug problems of some of its players in 1985. Tony Eason, the team's leader for five years, was cut. Veteran Steve Grogan has played for 15 years, long by NFL standards. Doug Flutie, a Heisman Trophy winner, has been inconsistent. And Marc Wilson, a fourth-string quarterback, has been cut by three teams.

There are bright spots though. Running back John Stephens is an established star. And linebacker Andre Tippett is considered by most experts to be as good as Lawrence Taylor. Cornerback Ronnie Lippett is one of the NFL's hardest hitters.

The Patriots won't be Super Bowl material for several more years. But Raymond Berry coaches the way he once played. He won't settle for anything less than the best.

READY FOR TAKEOFF

Quarterback Doug Flutie of the New England Patriots, shown here celebrating a win by his college team, Boston College.

Super Bowl III was the greatest game in the history of the New York Jets. They were underdogs to the powerful Baltimore Colts. Few people thought that the Jets had a chance to win the game.

"Broadway Joe" Namath was the New York quarterback. He didn't listen to anyone else. Namath predicted the Jets would win, then led them to a 16–7 victory.

Since that great day in history the Jets have faced tough times. In 1981 they had their first winning year since the 1969 Super Bowl season. In 1983 Joe Walton arrived as head coach and the Jets made the playoffs in 1985 and 1986.

Players like quarterback Ken O'Brien, wide receiver Al Toon and running back Freeman McNeil spark the Jets offense. Lineman Marty Lyons anchors the defense. But New York fans still talk more about former Jets like Namath, Don Maynard and Emerson Boozer than they do the current Jets. That's because the Jets are trying to rebuild their football team.

The Jets were originally named the New York Titans. Harry Wismer bought the team in 1959 and selected Sammy Baugh, a great NFL quarterback, as the team's first coach. In 1963 Wismer sold the Titans and the new owners renamed them the Jets. For many years the team played at Shea Stadium. They moved to the Meadowlands, in New Jersey, in 1984, where the New York Giants now play.

TIME LINE

1971—The Boston Patriots move to Foxboro and become the New England Patriots.

1976—The Patriots finish the year 11–3. They lose in the divisional playoffs to the Oakland Raiders, 24–21.

1978—The Houston Oilers dump New England in the divisional playoffs, 31–14.

1984—Raymond Berry becomes head coach.

1986—The Bears rip the Patriots, 46–10, in Super Bowl XX.

TIME LINE

1963—The New York Titans are renamed the New York Jets.

1965—Joe Namath signs a $427,000 contract.

1969—The Jets beat the Colts in Super Bowl III.

1977—Namath leaves the Jets for the Los Angeles Rams. After the season, he retires.

1981—The Jets have their first winning season in 12 years.

Former linebacker Marc Gastineau of the New York Jets sacks the Dolphins Dan Marino.

1985—The Jets lose to New England in the playoffs, 26–14.

1986—The Jets beat Kansas City, 35–15, in the wild-card game, but lose the next playoff game in overtime to Cleveland, 23–20.

CENTRAL DIVISION

Cincinnati Bengals
Cleveland Browns
Houston Oilers
Pittsburgh Steelers

THE ICKEY SHUFFLE

The Bengal tiger is one of the strongest, quickest and meanest animals in the world. Like their mascot, the Cincinnati Bengals want to be the strongest, meanest and toughest team in the NFL. They went to the Super Bowl twice during the 1980s but lost both times. That's something they want to change.

Ken Anderson, an outstanding quarterback, led the Bengals to the AFC championship and the Super Bowl in 1982. Six years later quarterback Boomer Esiason, the NFL's Most Valuable Player, took the Bengals to another championship game. Ironically it was the San Francisco 49ers who beat the Bengals in both of their Super Bowl appearances.

One thing is certain: The new Bengals are fun to follow. They have speedy receivers like Tim McGee and Eddie Brown, who make diving catches look easy. Ickey Woods ran for more than 1,000 yards in 1988 and invented the "Ickey Shuffle." The Ickey Shuffle is a dance that Ickey and Bengals fans do every time he scores a touchdown.

Running back Ickey Woods of the Cincinnati Bengals celebrating his team's 21–10 triumph over the Buffalo Bills in the 1989 AFC championship game.

Cincinnati was given an AFL franchise in 1967. The owner was Paul Brown, the former head coach of the Cleveland Browns. Brown named himself as the team's first coach. Under his leadership it took just four seasons for Cincinnati to win its first division championship.

After reaching the Super Bowl in 1982, Cincinnati fell on hard times. They finished second in their division three straight years. Then they dropped to a miserable fourth. Head coach Sam Wyche, who had taken over the Bengals in 1984, finally turned things around. He used a creative offense and the talents of Boomer Esiason to finish 14–5 in 1988.

TIME LINE

1970—Cincinnati wins the Central Division after losing its first seven games of the year.

1976—After 41 years as a coach, Paul Brown retires. He continues as owner and general manager.

1981—Bengals change their look. New uniforms and helmets have tiger stripes. They win the Central Division.

1982—Bengals fall to San Francisco, 26–21, in Super Bowl XVI.

1988—Bengals lose to San Francisco again, 20–16, in Super Bowl XXIII.

WHAT IS A BROWN?

What's a Cleveland Brown? In 1946 Arthur "Mickey" McBride started a team in the All-America Football Conference. He named Paul Brown head coach. Then McBride decided to have a contest to name the new team. Most of the people who entered the contest chose the name "Panthers." Brown didn't like that one. The second most popular choice was "Browns," after the new coach. Paul Brown didn't like that one either. But after a little pressure he accepted. The Cleveland Browns are the only team in the NFL who were named after a coach.

From the very beginning the Browns have been one of the greatest teams in football history. Immortal running back Jim Brown played nine seasons in Cleveland where he set many rushing records. Under their fiery head coach, the Browns won NFL championships in 1950, 1954, 1955 and 1964. Quarterback Otto Graham, a Hall of Famer, starred for the Browns in their glory days. Cleveland has won numerous Central Division titles but since the Super Bowl began in 1967, the Browns have not made a trip there.

But don't count the Browns out. Behind quarterback Bernie Kosar they have reached the playoffs four straight years since 1985. Durable wide receiver Webster Slaughter and running back Kevin Mack star on offense. Veteran Carl Hairston, cornerback Hanford Dixon and safety Thane Gash are defensive leaders. And rookie running back Eric Metcalf may be the NFL's brightest new star.

TIME LINE

1946—Paul Brown signs quarterback Otto Graham, one of the best to ever play the position.

1950—The Browns join the NFL and win the NFL championship during their first season in the league.

1961—Art Modell becomes the new Cleveland owner.

1963—Modell fires Paul Brown, who had problems getting along with players and management.

Cleveland's fans are among the loudest—and strangest—in all of professional football.

1986—Denver beats Cleveland, 23–20, in the AFC championship game in overtime.

1987—Denver does it again, beating the Browns 38–33 in the AFC championship game.

THE HOUSE OF PAIN

Their coach thinks singer Elvis Presley, who died in 1977, is really alive. Their ferocious players call their stadium "the House of Pain." And the Houston Oilers, who call themselves, "the Bad Boys," are quickly becoming one of the best teams in the NFL. Under head coach Jerry Glanville, the Oilers are known as a team that likes to have fun. Each week the guy who gets the biggest hit receives an army helmet. As for Elvis, Glanville has sometimes left free tickets at the box office for him—just in case he shows up.

But on Sunday afternoons Glanville and the Oilers mean business. They believe they are the meanest, toughest team in the NFL which is the way Glanville wants them. Glanville joined the Oilers in 1985 replacing Hugh Campbell as head coach. After rebuilding the team for two years the Oilers have made the playoffs every year since. And under Glanville they've never lost two games in a row.

Quarterback Warren Moon is a key reason for Houston's success. The backfield is led by former Heisman Trophy winner Mike Rozier and fullback Alonzo Highsmith. Two of Houston's wide receivers, Ernest Givins and Drew Hill, may be the best in the NFL.

K. S. "Bud" Adams started the Oilers in 1959. Houston won the AFL championship in 1960 and 1961 then lost the 1962 title game to the Dallas Texans in double overtime. In the 1970s the Oilers were successful under coach O. A. "Bum" Phillips. Bum was one of the most popular coaches in the NFL. Under Bum, the Oilers reached the playoffs three times. Each time they lost to the team that went on to win the Super Bowl.

Many great players have been with the Oilers. They include Earl Campbell, Ken Stabler, George Blanda and Billy "White Shoes" Johnson. Now with a blend of old and new talent, Jerry Glanville may need to leave tickets for the rest of his division. That might be the only way any other team gets to the playoffs!

Quarterback Warren Moon of the Houston Oilers

Until the 49ers won their fourth Super Bowl in 1990, the Steelers were the only NFL team ever to win four Super Bowl titles. Running back Rocky Bleier and receivers Lynn Swann and John Stallworth helped build the Pittsburgh dynasty. Defensive tackle "Mean" Joe Greene was the strength of the "steel curtain" defense, as the tough defensive line was called. Linebackers Jack Lambert and Jack Ham and defensive back Mel Blount were also among the greatest players in the game.

Today Noll is faced with the task of leading a new crop of Steelers back to the playoffs. He has numerous offensive tools like running back Tim Worley, receiver Louis Lipps and colorful quarter-

Quarterback Bubby Brister of the Pittsburgh Steelers

THE STEEL CURTAIN

Pro football has deep roots in Pittsburgh, Pennsylvania. Art Rooney, a legend among NFL owners, brought a team to Pittsburgh in 1933 and named them the Pirates after Pittsburgh's baseball team.

In 1940 the team's name was changed to the Steelers in honor of all the steel mills in Pittsburgh. Years later Rooney's Steelers dominated the NFL. It took a long, long time for them to become winners. But once they did, they were unstoppable. The Steelers won the Super Bowl in 1975, 1976, 1979 and 1980.

The turnaround came when the Steelers hired coach Chuck Noll in 1969. After a 1–13 season in 1970 Noll drafted quarterback Terry Bradshaw. Two years later running back Franco Harris joined the team. Together, Bradshaw, Harris and a great defense led the Steelers to the top of the NFL.

In Franco's rookie season Pittsburgh won the AFC Central. That was the first division title in the club's 39-year history. The famous "Immaculate Reception" gave them a playoff win.

Three years later Pittsburgh won Super Bowl IX over the Minnesota Vikings, 16–6. They followed that with a 21–17 win over the Dallas Cowboys in Super Bowl X. In Super Bowl XIII they won a rematch with Dallas, 35–31. They rolled over the Los Angeles Rams, 31–19, in Super Bowl XIV.

back Bubby Brister. In fact, Brister has offered his own guarantee that the Steelers will make it back to the Super Bowl. Brister has the Steelers and the city of Pittsburgh excited about the future. Noll is hoping that his experience and Brister's desire can make the Steelers great once more.

TIME LINE

1933—Art Rooney brings football to Pittsburgh for $2,500.

1940—The Pirates are renamed the Steelers in a newspaper contest.

1958—Quarterback Bobby Layne leads the Steelers best season in 11 years.

1969—Chuck Noll is hired as head coach.

1975—Super Bowl IX: Steelers 16, Vikings 6.

1976—Super Bowl X: Steelers 21, Cowboys 17.

1979—Super Bowl XIII: Steelers 35, Cowboys 31.

1980—Super Bowl XIV: Steelers 31, Rams 19.

1984—Steelers win their division.

WESTERN DIVISION

Denver Broncos
Kansas City Chiefs
Los Angeles Raiders
San Diego Chargers
Seattle Seahawks

MILE-HIGH HOPES

T he stadium where the Denver Broncos play their home games is named Mile-High Stadium, because the city of Denver is located high in a mountainous area. And like the name of their stadium, the

One of few bright moments for the Broncos in their Super Bowl history—recovering a Washington Redskins fumble in Super Bowl XXII.

Broncos have mile-high hopes of winning the Super Bowl despite losing it four times in the last 13 years.

In 1978 the Broncos were trampled by the Dallas Cowboys in Super Bowl XII by a score of 27–10. In 1987, with quarterback John Elway calling the signals, they lost Super Bowl XXI to the New York Giants 39–20. In 1988 the Washington Redskins beat them 42–10 in Super Bowl XXII, and in 1990 the San Francisco 49ers defeated the Broncos 55–10 in Super Bowl XXIV.

Despite those disappointing losses, few teams have experienced success as the Broncos have over the past five years. Part of the reason is scrambling quarterback John Elway, whose rifle arm and quick feet have made him one of the NFL's best. The Broncos traded for Elway in 1983 and offered him one of the biggest contracts ever— five years for $6 million. That was a lot of money but Elway hasn't let them down.

Elway likes to throw deep to speedy targets like Vance Johnson, Mark Jackson and Ricky Nattiel, who the fans call "the Three Amigos." Hard-hitting safety Steve Atwater and linebacker Karl Mecklenburg anchor the Denver defense.

The Broncos were one of the original teams in the AFL. They were started by a man and his son, Lee and Bob Howsam, in 1959. Denver went through some tough times early on—winning didn't come easily. Finally, under coach Red Miller, the Broncos won their first AFC Western Division title in 1977.

In 1981 Dan Reeves became head coach. Reeves had spent his whole career as a player and coach with the Dallas Cowboys. A brilliant play-caller, Reeves has molded the Broncos into one of the most respected teams in the AFC. Since Dan came aboard they've made the playoffs every season except one.

TIME LINE

1967—The Broncos are the first AFL team to win a game against an NFL team when they beat the Detroit Lions in a pre-season game.

1968—A minor-league baseball stadium is renovated and given to the city of Denver. It is officially renamed "Denver Mile-High Stadium."

1976—Every available ticket is sold. It's the team's seventh sell-out season. Every year since, every game of the Broncos has been a sell-out.

1978—The Broncos lose Super Bowl XII, 27–10, to the Dallas Cowboys.

1986—The Giants beat Denver, 39–10, in Super Bowl XXI.

1987—Washington trounces Denver, 42–10, in Super Bowl XXII.

ON THE WARPATH

Lamar Hunt had a big idea. The millionaire from Texas wanted to bring an NFL team to Dallas. When he couldn't pull it off he started a new league.

The American Football League began in 1959 with six teams. One of those teams was an AFL version of the Dallas Texans, a team that had moved to Baltimore seven years earlier. After Hunt got his team together, the NFL created the Dallas Cowboys. But Hunt and the Texans had trouble drawing a crowd. The Dallas fans paid more attention to the NFL's Cowboys. So Hunt moved his team to Kansas City and renamed it the Chiefs.

Coach Hank Stram made the Chiefs winners. He drafted Heisman Trophy winner Mike Garrett in 1966. The Chiefs won their division that year. Kansas City won the AFL title in 1967 but lost to the Green Bay Packers in the first Super Bowl. The Chiefs won their only Super Bowl in 1970 over the Minnesota Vikings behind quarterback Len Dawson. Other members of the championship Chiefs were running back Ed Podolak and wide receiver Otis Taylor.

Since its Super Bowl victory, the Chiefs have made the playoffs only twice, in 1972 and 1986. But new coach Marty Schottenheimer hopes to change all that. Schottenheimer spent five seasons with the Cleveland Browns where he put them in the playoffs four times and the AFC championship game twice, then joined the Chiefs in 1989.

The Chiefs have excellent players too, like running back Christian Okoye, wide receiver Stephone Paige and linebacker Derrick Thomas. With Schottenheimer leading them the Chiefs will soon make it into the playoffs.

TIME LINE

1962—Chiefs win AFL championship over the Houston Oilers.

1970—Running back Mike Garrett is traded to San Diego.

1971—On Christmas Day the Chiefs lose a playoff game to the Miami Dolphins, 27–24, in the NFL's longest game ever: 82 minutes and 40 seconds.

1974—The Chiefs suffer through their first losing season in 11 years. After 15 years as head coach, Hank Stram is fired.

1981—Marv Levy coaches the Chiefs to their first winning season in eight years.

1986—The Chiefs reach the playoffs for the first time since 1971.

1989—Marty Schottenheimer replaces Frank Gansz as head coach.

Running back Christian Okoye of the Kansas City Chiefs

PRIDE AND POISE

For years the silver and black of the Raiders have been recognized as winning colors. But it wasn't that way in the beginning. In 1960 the city of Oakland, California was awarded an AFL franchise. The Raiders had trouble even finding a place to play and when they did take the field, they weren't a pretty sight.

Al Davis became Oakland's fourth head coach in 1963. He reorganized the Raiders and guided them to their first winning season. He left the team in 1966 but came back a year later as the team's owner. Davis changed the team's attitude and image. He wanted a big, dominating football team, and soon the Raiders turned into the NFL's original bad boys.

In 1967 the Raiders began to dominate their opposition. They won the AFL championship, then followed that with a trip to Super Bowl II, where they lost to the Green Bay Packers, 33–14. By 1976 the Raiders had won 9 AFC West titles in 10 years.

Under coach John Madden, the Raiders won Super Bowl XI in 1977. Coach Tom Flores guided them to wins in Super Bowl XV in 1981 and Super Bowl XVIII in 1984. In 1982 the Raiders had their first losing record in 19 years and Davis moved them to Los Angeles.

Former Raider All-Pro Art Shell became the NFL's first black head coach in 1989. Shell is trying to regain the enthusiasm of the old Raiders and he has tremendous talent with which to work. Heisman Trophy winners Marcus Allen, Bo Jackson and Tim Brown give the Raiders awesome offensive power. Wide receiver Willie Gault is one of the fastest men in the NFL. Defensively, linemen Bill Pickel and Howie Long and safety Vann McElroy are dominating stars.

But these guys have a lot to live up to. They're following in the footsteps of some of the NFL's greatest players—guys like quarterbacks Daryle Lamonica, George Blanda, Jim Plunkett and Ken "the Snake" Stabler, wide receiver Fred Biletnikoff, tight end Dave Casper and defensive backs Willie Brown and Lester Hayes.

In recent years the Raiders haven't matched their earlier triumphs. They haven't won the AFC West since 1985. But their motto is "Pride and Poise: A Commitment to Excellence." With an ex-Raider like Art Shell leading the team, a return to glory doesn't seem too far away.

CHARGER POWER

Barron Hilton, the same man who started the Hilton hotel chain, started the San Diego Chargers in 1959. The Chargers were one of the AFL's first six teams. Los Angeles was their original home before they moved up the coast to San Diego in 1961.

From the beginning the Chargers were a strong team. They won the AFL Western Division several times in their early years. In 1961 Hilton moved the team to San Diego. They won the AFL championship by defeating the Boston Patriots in 1964.

Great quarterbacks are a San Diego tradition. Dan Fouts played 15 seasons with the Chargers. He led them to the playoffs three consecutive years, from 1979 through 1981. Fouts holds all of the Chargers passing records. He followed

Former head coach John Madden of the then-Oakland Raiders

Former quarterback Dan Fouts of the San Diego Chargers

TIME LINE

1967—The Raiders defeat the Houston Oilers for the AFL championship but lose to the Green Bay Packers, 33–14, in Super Bowl II.

1969—John Madden becomes head coach.

1976—George Blanda retires after a 26-year NFL career.

1977—Oakland whips Minnesota, 32–14, in Super Bowl XI.

1981—Oakland beats the Eagles, 27–10, in Super Bowl XV.

1982—The Raiders move from Oakland to Los Angeles.

1984—The Raiders beat the Redskins, 38–9, in Super Bowl XVIII.

1989—Art Shell becomes the NFL's first black head coach.

another fine passer, John Hadl. Johnny Unitas, the great Baltimore Colts quarterback, played his last games in the NFL with the Chargers.

Zany Jim McMahon and Billy Joe Tolliver, were San Diego's quarterbacks. McMahon is wild and unpredictable, but he can throw a football. With targets like speedy Anthony Miller, San Diego's passing attack could be very dangerous.

Miller follows in the footsteps of great receivers like Kellen Winslow and Charlie Joiner, two of the best in NFL history. Joiner is second in the league in career-pass receptions and yardage. Winslow was a tight end who is best remembered for his amazing courage in a playoff game against the Dolphins in 1982. He caught 13 passes for 166 yards and blocked a punt in that game.

Dan Henning took over the Chargers coaching duties in 1989. Henning, who played for the Chargers in 1964, has coached with several teams. He is looking for leadership from McMahon and other veteran charger players to put the charge back in the San Diego attack.

TIME LINE

1959—Barron Hilton founds the Chargers in Los Angeles.

1961—Hilton moves the Chargers to San Diego.

1973—Johnny Unitas plays three games for the Chargers and retires from football.

1975—The Chargers finish 2–12. It's the worst season in the team's history.

1979—The Chargers win their first division championship in 14 years.

1988—After 15 seasons Dan Fouts retires.

THE BOZ

The city of Seattle was chosen for an NFL team in 1974. The Seahawks got their name when 151 people chose it over other suggestions. Lloyd W. Nordstrom led a group of Seattle businessmen who paid $16 million to buy the team. Jack Patera of the Minnesota Vikings was named the team's first coach in 1976.

The Seahawks were mildly successful from the start. But they became perennial playoff challengers after Chuck Knox was hired to coach the Seahawks in 1983. Knox's Seahawks made the playoffs for the first time in 1984 and have been back twice since then. In 1987 they lost an overtime game to Houston. In 1988 they fell to the Cincinnati Bengals, 21–13.

Wide receiver Steve Largent holds five NFL all-time receiving records including receptions and yardage. Largent joined the Seahawks in 1976. Since then he's rewritten the record books, becoming the best receiver in NFL history. Quarterback Dave Krieg and powerful running backs Curt Warner and John L. Williams are three more of Seattle's offensive stars.

When the Seahawks drafted cocky linebacker Brian "the Boz" Bosworth, they expected great things. He sports an earring and a good-looking haircut. There's even been a book written about him. And he's got great talent. Despite his reputation as a tough linebacker, Bosworth has been seriously hampered by injuries throughout his career. The Seahawks are counting on Bosworth and fellow linebacker Tony Woods to lead their defense.

Chuck Knox is one of the NFL's best coaches. He wins. Knox has brought the Seahawks a long way since taking over but he's still not satisfied.

Linebacker Brian Bosworth of the Seattle Seahawks

TIME LINE

1974—Seattle is awarded an NFL franchise.

1978—The Seahawks finish with a winning record, 9–7.

1984—The Seahawks beat the Los Angeles Raiders in their first playoff appearance before losing to the Miami Dolphins.

1987—Seattle loses to Houston in the playoffs, 23–20.

1988—Seattle loses to Cincinnati in the playoffs, 21–13.

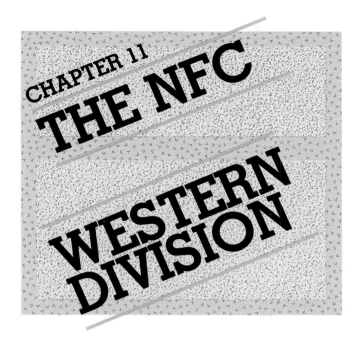

Atlanta Falcons
Los Angeles Rams
New Orleans Saints
San Francisco 49ers

PRIME TIME

"Neon" Deion Sanders lights up game day in Atlanta. Also known as "Prime Time," Sanders is a swaggering, speedy cornerback. He and the rest of the Falcons have youth on their side. They've got an attitude.

Along with Sanders, the Falcons have nose tackle Tony Casillas, linebacker Aundray Bruce and cornerback Scott Case on a defense that should be one of the best in the NFL. In 1988 Case led the NFL in interceptions with 10. Bruce and Casillas were both Number 1 draft picks. Quarterback Chris Miller is a star of the future while running back John Settle is a rugged, straight-ahead runner.

With so much young talent the Falcons are trying to shake off the memory of many losing seasons. The last time the Falcons had a winning record was in 1982 when they made it to the playoffs.

In 1965 both the AFL and the NFL wanted to start a team in Atlanta. The people of the city were the first to be able to choose their league,
and they chose the NFL. Rankin Smith bought the team and still owns it today.

The Falcons were named in a contest sponsored by an Atlanta radio station. It was hoped the team would show the courage and fighting spirit of the bird and become winners in the NFL. The team had plenty of courage but winning has been difficult.

The Falcons made their first playoff appearance in 1978, 13 years after they began. They won the division in 1980 and lost a playoff thriller to the Dallas Cowboys. Their 1982 playoff appearance was brief with an opening loss to the Minnesota Vikings.

But the Falcons believe their worst days are over. Their commitment to youth could mean better times ahead.

Running back Deion Sanders of the Atlanta Falcons

1965—The people of Atlanta choose the NFL as the league for their new team.

1978—In their first playoff appearance, the Falcons defeat the Philadelphia Eagles in the wild-card game, 14–13, but then lose to the Dallas Cowboys, 27–20.

1980—Atlanta loses again to the Cowboys in the playoffs, 30–27.

1982—Minnesota beats the Falcons in the playoffs, 30–24.

CALIFORNIA DREAMIN'

"Wild rams butt heads harder than any other animal," said Homer Marshman, the first owner of the Rams. That was true of his team in 1937 and it's still true today.

The Rams began in Cleveland. They won the NFL championship in 1945 and took their head-butting style of play to the West Coast. In 1951 they won the NFL title by whipping the Browns, the team that replaced them in Cleveland.

Since then, the Rams have established a reputation for one thing: winning. Virtually every year they are in contention for the playoffs. In 1980 the Rams reached Super Bowl XIV where they lost to the Pittsburgh Steelers, 31–19. Though they haven't won an NFL championship in nearly 40 years the Rams haven't been afraid to butt heads with any team on Sunday afternoon.

Merlin Olsen, Deacon Jones, Lamar Lundy and Rosey Grier were the Ram players who chewed up running backs in the 1960s. They became known as the "Fearsome Foursome." Over a 10-year period, Roman Gabriel led the offense at quarterback. In 1974 James Harris became the first black quarterback to led a team to a championship when the Rams won their division. That title was one of eight in a row that Los Angeles captures from 1973 to 1980.

In 1983 they began a string of four straight playoff appearances. The Rams hired John Robinson from the University of Southern California as head coach that same year. Robinson is now the winningest coach in the Rams' history. His team has missed the playoffs only once in his first six years.

In 1987 the Rams traded Eric Dickerson, one of the NFL's best rushers ever. Dickerson broke O. J. Simpson's season rushing record while he played for the Rams. But because the Rams couldn't

Quarterback Jim Everett of the Los Angeles Rams

seem to make Dickerson happy, they traded him to the Indianapolis Colts. The Rams got a total of six first- and second-round draft choices for Dickerson.

They're using those picks to build a powerhouse that already includes 6' 5", 225-pound quarterback Jim Everett. Everett holds the team records for touchdown passes and yardage in a single season. Receivers like Ron Brown and Henry Ellard are lightning-fast targets. On defense, linebacker Kevin Greene is a fierce pass rusher.

Los Angeles and San Francisco battle it out regularly for the NFC West crown. Robinson has the Rams in shape for the next showdown.

TIME LINE

1937—Homer Marshman founds the Rams in Cleveland, Ohio.

1945—The Rams win the NFL championship over the Washington Redskins.

1951—The Rams defeat the Cleveland Browns for a second NFL title.

1957—Future NFL commissioner Pete Rozelle becomes general manager.

1966—George Allen becomes head coach.

1973—The Rams win the first of their eight NFC West championships.

THE SAINTS ARE MARCHIN' IN

It's tough to win in New Orleans. Part of the problem is that the Saints play in the toughest division in football—the NFC West—along with the Rams and 49ers. The Saints got their name from the popular Dixieland jazz tune "When the Saints Go Marching In." In 1966 John W. Mecom, Jr., became the largest shareholder in the new organization.

From the beginning New Orleans has been the downfall of many great coaches. Hank Stram, who won a Super Bowl with the Chiefs, couldn't win in New Orleans. Bum Phillips, who took many Houston teams to the playoffs, couldn't either. Then head Coach Jim Mora came to New Orleans in 1986 after coaching the USLF's Philadelphia Stars to all three USFL championship games and winning two of them. He also won more games than any other coach in the three-year history of the USFL.

Jim Mora likes championship games. In 1987 the Saints reached the playoffs for the first time ever. It was just a wild-card game and the Minnesota Vikings ripped them, 44–10. But it was still the playoffs. At the time, the Saints were the only team in the history of the NFL that *hadn't* been to the playoffs.

Quarterback Bobby Hebert of the New Orleans Saints

The Saints don't believe in quitting. They believe they are finally on a steady path to improvement. Veteran quarterback Bobby Hebert sets up in a backfield that includes a pair of tough, talented running backs—Reuben Mayes and Dalton Hilliard. Hebert was nicknamed the "Cajun Cannon" in college at Northwestern Louisiana. (Cajuns are Louisianans descended from French-speaking immigrants from Acadia, in eastern Canada.) Linebackers Pat Swilling, Sam Mills, Rickey Jackson and Vaughan Johnson lead a top-ranked defense.

The Saints have had 10 head coaches in their history. Jim Mora has already outlasted the average New Orleans coach's term of two years. Many believe that Mora simply needs time to chip away at the division's long-standing powerhouses, the 49ers and the Rams.

TIME LINE

1966—New Orleans is granted an NFL team. John W. Mecom, Jr., is the majority owner.

1970—Tom Dempsey, born without a right hand and no toes on his right foot, kicks an NFL record 63-yard field goal against the Detroit Lions.

1975—The Louisiana Superdome becomes the Saints' new home.

1980—The Saints finish a horrible season at 1–15.

1986—Tom Benson purchases the team. Jim Mora is named head coach; Jim Finks is named general manager.

1987—In their first playoff appearance, the Saints lose the wild-card game to Minnesota, 44–10.

THE TEAM OF THE EIGHTIES

When Joe Montana found John Taylor for the winning touchdown in Super Bowl XXII, the San Francisco 49ers became more than just world champions. They became a part of history.

If the Chicago Bears was the team of the '40s, the Green Bay packers was the team of the '60s and the Pittsburgh Steelers was the team of the '70s, the 49ers was definitely the team of the '80s. Without a doubt, they were the best of the decade and quite possible the best ever.

Quarterback Montana and fellow superstars Jerry Rice and Roger Craig have made the 49ers almost unbeatable in recent years. Montana has proved himself as the best quarterback in the NFL. In Super Bowl XXIII, he engineered the winning 92-yard drive that beat Cincinnati in the final seconds. He's calm under pressure, making the call that counts and spotting the open man. Usually the open man is Rice, a crafty veteran receiver at the top of his game. When Craig runs the ball, he's an awesome combination of quickness and muscle.

The 49ers won three Super Bowls in the 1980s. They beat the Bengals twice, in 1982 and 1989. In 1985 San Francisco whipped the Miami Dolphins in Super Bowl XIX, 38–16. Montana was named MVP in two of the games and Rice in the third.

When coach Bill Walsh went out on top in 1989 ending a nine-year career at the 49ers helm, assistant coach George Seifert took control. Walsh was a tough act to follow but the team kicked off the new decade by defeating the Denver Broncos 55–10 in Super Bowl XXIV. Seifert still has the offensive fire power and a defensive unit that includes All-Pro safety Ronnie Lott and cornerback Eric Wright.

The team that made the 1980s its own almost didn't get the chance to play in the NFL. When Anthony J. Morabito, E. J. Turre and Allen E. Sorrell were denied an NFL franchise, they joined the All-American Football Conference. Three years later, in 1949, San Francisco was admitted to the NFL.

Turre and Sorrell named the 49ers after the horde of gold prospectors who flocked to California in 1849, during the Gold Rush, when gold was discovered in some of the streams in northern California. But when the 49ers began prospecting for wins they came up empty-handed for almost 25 years. The first NFC West championship for San Francisco was in 1970. The 49ers then won division titles in the next two years. But all three times they were beaten by the Dallas Cowboys in the NFC championship game.

San Francisco hit an all-time low with a 2–14 record in 1978. Then in came Walsh the following year, and soon the 49ers were winning world titles.

Former head coach Bill Walsh of the San Francisco 49ers

TIME LINE

1946—Anthony J. Morabito forms the San Francisco 49ers and enters the All-American Football Conference.

1949—The NFL accepts the 49ers.

1951—San Francisco acquires star quarterback Y. A. Tittle.

1960—Coach Howard "Red" Hickey begins using the shotgun formation on offense.

1970—The 49ers win the first NFC West championship in their 25-year history.

1979—Bill Walsh becomes head coach.

1982—Super Bowl XVI: 49ers 26, Bengals 21.

1985—Super Bowl XIX: 49ers 38, Dolphins 16.

1989—Super Bowl XXIII: 49ers 20, Bengals 16.

1990—Super Bowl XXIV: 49ers 55, Broncos 10.

CENTRAL DIVISION

Chicago Bears
Detroit Lions
Green Bay Packers
Minnesota Vikings
Tampa Bay Buccaneers

MONSTERS OF THE MIDWAY

Sixty years ago a young man named George Halas had a good, steady job. He worked for A. E. Staley, a starch manufacturer in Decatur, Illinois. Then his boss asked him to organize the company's football team. And the company actually paid him for it!

In 1921 Halas and the Chicago Staleys were champions of the American Professional Football Association. The next year the team moved to Chicago and Halas became an owner. Since the Staleys played at Cub Park, the home of the city's baseball team, Halas renamed his team the Bears in 1922. He also persuaded the APFA to change its name to the National Football League.

When Halas signed Harold "Red" Grange to play for the Bears in 1925, he brought the NFL its first superstar. In the 1930s and 1940s the Bears became the top team in the league winning its championship six times. The 1940 title game was a milestone. The Bears whipped the Washington Redskins, 73–0, the largest margin of victory ever in the NFL.

After four different periods as the Bears coach, Halas retired in 1968 with a record of 320–147–30. He remains the NFL's winningest coach. Under Halas, the Bears earned the nickname "Monsters of the Midway" for their crushing style of play. (The Midway is part of downtown

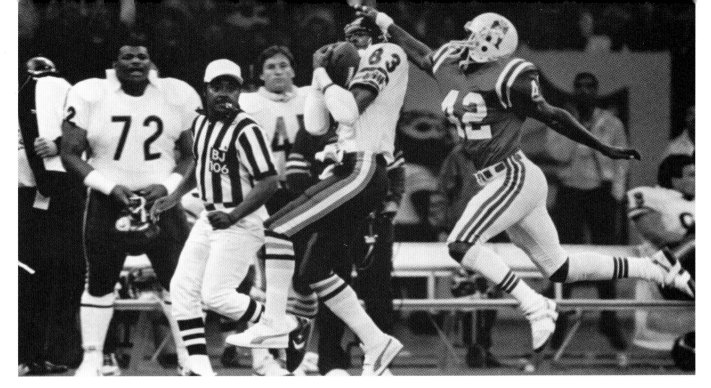

Receiver Willie Gault of the Chicago Bears

Chicago.) Affectionately known as "Papa Bear," Halas died in 1983.

Several of the NFL's legends, including Grange, Sid Luckman, Gayle Sayers, Walter Payton, Dick Butkus and Mike Ditka became famous with the Bears. The fist-pounding Ditka became the team's head coach in 1982. Twenty-three years ago after their last NFL championship he led them to victory in Super Bowl XX in 1986.

Today Ditka depends on the leadership of players like middle linebacker Mike Singletary and quarterbacks Mike Tomczak and Jim Harbaugh. Neal Anderson is a solid running back. Linemen Steve McMichael, Richard Dent, William "the Refrigerator" Perry and Dan Hampton are the Bears teeth on defense. For Mike Ditka getting on top wasn't enough. He wants to stay there.

TIME LINE

1920—The Chicago Bears are begun as the Decatur Staleys and are coached by George Halas.

1925—Halas gains public attention when he signs Harold "Red" Grange to play for the Bears.

1940—The Bears defeat the Washington Redskins, 73–0, in the NFL championship.

1968—At 73, Halas retires for the final time as Chicago head coach. His record is 320–147–30.

1969—The Bears finish 1–13, last in the league.

1982—Mike Ditka becomes head coach.

1983—George "Papa Bear" Halas dies.

1986—Super Bowl XX: Bears 46, Patriots 10.

RESTORE THE ROAR

There has been nothing to brag about in Detroit since a division title in 1983. But coach Wayne Fontes is hoping to "Restore the Roar" with the Lions. That's why he hired innovative offensive coaches Darrel "Mouse" Davis and June Jones.

Fontes knows Davis and Jones believe in wide-open football. No offense in the league is as much fun to watch as Davis's invention, the run-and-shoot. Unleashed on the NFL for the first time in 1989 the run 'n' shoot at times was unstoppable. Once he gets the players he needs, Mouse believes he can make the Lions roar again.

Running back Barry Sanders, winner of the Heisman Trophy in 1988, came to the Lions from Oklahoma State and has given the team a major boost. They also helped themselves in 1988 with the signing of quarterback Rodney Peete. And wide receiver Richard Johnson proved he was better than anybody the Lions had ever had. As these guys learn the run-and-shoot, Fontes is expecting fireworks. Linebackers Mike Cofer, Chris Spielman and George Jamison lead a young, hard-hitting Detroit defense.

The Lions date back to 1934 when George Richards, a radio station owner, went shopping for a football team. He found the Portsmouth (Ohio) Spartans who had joined the NFL in 1930. Richards paid $21,500 for the team and moved it to Detroit.

Once there, Richards held a contest to rename his team. The winner chose "Lions" so the football team would be the "King of Beasts" over the Tigers, Detroit's baseball team. After years of trying, the Lions won back-to-back NFL championships in 1952 and 1953. They beat the Cleveland Browns twice to win the titles.

These days Coach Fontes and his staff want more than just wins. They want an exciting brand of football in Detroit. Once the run-and-shoot hits full speed, better times are just around the corner.

Running back Barry Sanders of the Detroit Lions

TIME LINE

1934—George Richards buys the Portsmouth Spartans. He moves the team to Detroit and renames it the Lions.

1949—The Lions finish fourth in the league. It's the first time since 1945 that they're out of the cellar.

1952—NFL champions over the Cleveland Browns.

1953—Second straight NFL championship. Cleveland is the victim again.

1962—The Lions win 11 games, the most in one season in their history.

1967—The Lions fall to the Denver Broncos, the first NFL team to lose to an AFL team.

1975—The Lions make the Pontiac Silverdome their home stadium.

1988—Wayne Fontes is hired as head coach.

THE PACK IS BACK

Back in 1919 when Earl "Curly" Lambeau talked the Indian Packing Company into a $500 sponsorship for a professional football team, he had no idea what the future would bring. Lambeau's home was Green Bay, Wisconsin. He named his team the Green Bay Packers in honor of the company's donation.

The Green Bay team dominated the NFL of the 1930s. Player-coach Lambeau led them to the NFL championship in 1930, 1931, 1936 and 1939.

Offensive tackle Tony Mandarich of the Green Bay Packers

The Packers of the 1960s and Coach Vince Lombardi became legendary. Greats like Bart Starr, Paul Hornung, Jim Taylor and Ray Nitschke made it happen and Lombardi was the driving, inspirational force behind them.

The glory of the Lombardi era is only a memory now and Coach Lindy Infante, who joined the team in 1988, has a great tradition to live up to. Others have tried and failed. But the Pack is back.

The Packers paid a high price for offensive tackle Tony Mandarich. They did it because they believe it's an investment in their future. Behind quarterback Don "Magic Man" Majkowski and first-round draft pick Brent Fullwood at running back, the Packers are hot on the playoff trail. Young linebacker Tim Harris is the best in the NFL right now. He and safety Mark Murphy anchor an improving defense.

The Packers, who have built a reputation for winning games in their final seconds, are slowly gaining momentum. If history repeats itself, the other teams in the NFL are in for trouble.

TIME LINE

1919—Earl "Curly" Lambeau starts a pro football team with support from the Indian Packing Company.

1930—Green Bay wins its first NFL championship.

1944—Packers win their only NFL crown in the 1940s.

1950—After 31 years with the Packers, Curly Lambeau resigns.

1959—Vince Lombardi begins a new era as Green Bay coach.

1961—Green Bay wins its first NFL championship in 17 years.

1967—Super Bowl I: Packers 35, Chiefs 10.

1968—Super Bowl II: Packers 33, Raiders 14.

1969—Lombardi leaves the Packers.

1988—Lindy Infante becomes Green Bay head coach following a series of unsuccessful Lombardi followers.

The immortal Vince Lombardi became Packers coach in 1959. From the beginning Lombardi made sure the team knew who was boss. As the players' respect for their coach grew so did the number of wins each season. "Winning isn't everything. It's the only thing," Lombardi told the Packers.

The Packers would settle for nothing less than victory. Lombardi's motivation made them believe in themselves. In 1961 Green Bay won its first NFL championship in 22 years. They went on to manhandle the competition in the 1960s just as they had three decades earlier.

The Green Bay dynasty claimed NFL championships in 1962, 1965, 1966, 1967 and 1968. A new sports event of spectacular size, the Super Bowl, appeared in 1967. The Packers beat the Kansas City Chiefs 35–10 for bragging rights in the AFL–NFL rivalry. In Super Bowl II, Lombardi's Packers whipped the AFL's Oakland Raiders, 33–14.

LARGE AND IN CHARGE

It's O.K. to feel a little sorry for one team in the NFL. The Minnesota Vikings have reached the Super Bowl four times only to lose every time. But though they have been unable to win the big one, they are an established force in the NFC.

The Vikings owned the NFC Central Division in the 1970s, winning eight titles. Scrambling quarterback Fran Tarkenton and punishing runner Chuck Foreman were Minnesota offensive greats. Linemen Jim Marshall, Alan Page and Carl Eller with safety Paul Krause led a defense that became known as the "Purple People Eaters."

In 1970 the Vikings made their first Super Bowl appearance. They lost to the Kansas City Chiefs, 23–7, in Super Bowl IV. In back-to-back losses, the Vikings fell to the Miami Dolphins, 24–7, and the Pittsburgh Steelers, 16–6, in Super Bowls VIII and IX. In 1977 the Oakland Raiders handed them a 32–14 defeat in Super Bowl XI. In the Vikings first 20 years in the NFL they made the playoffs 11 times.

The current Vikings are large and in charge of the NFC Central. Behind quarterback Wade Wilson, wide receiver Anthony Carter, running back Herschel Walker and defensive linemen Keith Millard and Chris Doleman, the Vikings control their own destiny. (Walker was acquired from the Dallas Cowboys midway through the 1989 season in exchange for four draft picks and more than $3 million!) Head coach Jerry Burns was an assistant to former Vikings coach Bud Grant in all four Minnesota Super Bowls. He also worked under Vince Lombardi when the Packers won two Super Bowls.

TIME LINE

1960—The Vikings are created in Minnesota when Max Winter gains a franchise.

1968—Minnesota wins its first division championship.

1970—Super Bowl IV: Chiefs 23, Vikings 7.

1974—Super Bowl VIII: Dolphins 24, Vikings 7.

Quarterback Fran Tarkenton of the Minnesota Vikings

1975—Super Bowl IX: Steelers 16, Vikings 6.

1977—Super Bowl XI: Raiders 32, Vikings 14.

1979—Superstar quarterback Fran Tarkenton retires.

1986—Assistant Coach Jerry Burns is named head coach.

1987—Vikings lose to Washington Redskins in NFC championship game.

1989—Vikings acquire superstar running back Herschel Walker.

ON THE WAY IN TAMPA BAY

In its most recent round of expansion, the NFL awarded a franchise to a second Florida city (Miami was the first) in 1974. Hugh F. Culverhouse paid $16 million to the league, and the Bucs stopped in Tampa Bay. The

In 1981 and 1983 the Bucs again won their division championship. Then they slid back down to the bottom. They had the worst record in the NFL in 1985. In recent seasons they've struggled to stay out of the cellar.

Ray Perkins left the University of Alabama in 1987 to coach the Buccaneers. With Heisman Trophy winner Vinny Testaverde of the University of Miami at quarterback and rugged William Howard running the football, Tampa Bay is slowly building a powerful attack. But it will take time before the Buccaneers are sailing the high seas again.

Former head coach Tom Landry of the Dallas Cowboys

Quarterback Vinny Testaverde of the Tampa Bay Buccaneers

new owner headed a committee that chose the name Buccaneers from 400 suggestions provided by the public.

Few people expected the Buccaneers to challenge in the NFC Central their first year out. In fact they were the first team in the NFL ever to go 0–14. They didn't even score in five of the losses. The Bucs lost 12 straight games the next year before snapping their 26-game losing streak against the New Orleans Saints in 1977.

John McKay left his successful job at the University of Southern California to become Tampa's first head coach. By 1979 his team had gone from a winless joke to the champions of the NFC Central Division. In their best season ever, they lost the NFC championship game to the Los Angeles Rams by a score of 9–0.

TIME LINE

1974—Hugh F. Culverhouse becomes owner of the NFL's Tampa Bay expansion team.

1976—In the worst performance in NFL history, the Buccaneers finish a dismal 0–14.

1977—Tampa Bay snaps a 26-game losing streak with a win over the New Orleans Saints.

1979—The Bucs win the NFC Central division title.

1980—The Bucs lose the NFC title game to the L.A. Rams, 9–0.

1981—The Bucs win their division.

1983—The Bucs win their division.

1985—Tampa Bay finishes with the worst record in the league.

1986—The Bucs make Bo Jackson the first pick in the draft. Jackson chooses baseball instead.

1987—Ray Perkins is named head coach.

Dallas Cowboys
New York Giants
Philadelphia Eagles
Phoenix Cardinals
Washington Redskins

AMERICA'S TEAM

February 25, 1989, marked the end of an era in Dallas. Tom Landry, the only coach the team had ever had, left the Cowboys after 28 years with a record of 270-178-6. Landry had guided Dallas from its expansion days to two Super Bowl championships. With Landry gone, Jimmy Johnson came to Dallas from the University of Miami. Management had replaced Landry but it couldn't replace the memories.

The Dallas Cowboys were founded in 1960 as the NFL's answer to the Dallas Texans of the AFL. Almost immediately the Cowboys got most of the fan support so Texans owner Lamar Hunt moved his team to Kansas City and renamed it the Chiefs.

In their seventh year the Cowboys were already a force in the NFL. The Green Bay Packers, an NFL powerhouse, edged Dallas, 21–17, in the 1967 NFL championship game. Played in 13-degrees-below-zero temperatures, the classic game became known as the "Ice Bowl."

In their relatively short history the Cowboys have reached the Super Bowl five times. The team won Super Bowl VI by beating the Miami Dolphins, 24–3, in 1972 and Super Bowl XII by beating Denver Broncos, 27–10, in 1978, but lost a heartbreaker in 1971 in Super Bowl V to the Baltimore Colts, 16–13. In Super Bowls X and XIII the Cowboys were runners-up to the Pittsburgh Steelers.

The scrambling of quarterback Roger Staubach gave NFL fans some of their greatest memories. His famous "Hail Mary" pass to Drew Pearson beat the Minnesota Vikings, 17–14, in the 1975 playoffs. Fans learned never to count out "Roger the Dodger."

Dallas had its share of great players. For many years, running back Tony Dorsett ran through, around and over tacklers and set numerous rushing records in Dallas. At one time, defensive tackles Bob Lilly and Randy White and linebackers Chuck Howley and Lee Roy Jordan made the Cowboys' "Doomsday Defense" one of the NFL's best. The Cowboys eventually became known as "America's Team."

Despite having the NFL's worst record in 1989 Johnson remains committed to improving with young players. Offensively, wide receiver Michael Irvin and quarterback Troy Aikman give Dallas a deep threat.

The fans in Dallas are accustomed to winning and the Cowboys have a fantastic tradition. Johnson and his team must deliver.

TIME LINE

1960—The Cowboys are founded in Dallas. Tom Landry is named head coach.

1967—Dallas loses to Green Bay in the famous "Ice Bowl."

1971—Super Bowl V: Colts 16, Cowboys 13.

1972—Super Bowl VI: Cowboys 24, Dolphins 3.

1976—Super Bowl X: Steelers 21, Cowboys 17.

1978—Super Bowl XII: Cowboys 27, Broncos 17.

1979—Super Bowl XIII: Steelers 35, Cowboys 31.

1984—Cowboys are out of the playoffs for the first time in 10 years.

1989—The Cowboys are sold to oil man Jerry Jones. Tom Landry is replaced as coach after 28 years. Jimmy Johnson, who won a national championship at the University of Miami, is named head coach.

THE LAND OF GIANTS

The New York Giants burst back into professional football history in 1986 when they roared through the regular season with a 14–2 record and defeated the Denver Broncos in Super Bowl XX. It was their first championship in 30 years, but a lot of people forgot that the Giants are rich with history and had been a giant among NFL teams for many years.

In 1925 Timothy J. Mara paid $2,500 to start the Giants. He named the team after New York's pro baseball team. Then he brought Jim Thorpe, probably the greatest athlete of all time, to play on his first team. In just two years the Giants became the 1927 NFL champions. They also won the NFL title in 1934, 1938 and 1956.

The 1934 championship contest is remembered as the "Sneakers Game." In freezing conditions, the Giants beat the Chicago Bears. Some of their players wore basketball sneakers to give them better footing on the icy playing field.

Along with Thorpe, other memorable Giants of the past include Y. A. Tittle, Frank Gifford, Fran Tarkenton and Pat Summerall. Tittle threw for more touchdowns in a single season than any other Giants quarterback. Gifford still holds the Giants records for career touchdowns and receiving yards. He and Summerall are now successful sports broadcasters for ABC and CBS.

Since winning the championship in 1986, several players have left the team. But steady quarterback Phil Simms, wide receiver Lionel Manuel and running back Joe Morris still lead the offensive attack. And of course linebacker Lawrence Taylor, who has played his way into the record books, still inspires his teammates with hard-nosed, all-out football.

TIME LINE

1925—Timothy J. Mara buys the rights to a New York franchise for $2,500.

1927—The Giants win their first NFL championship.

1930—The Giants win the first of eight Eastern Division championships in the 1930s.

1934—In the "Sneakers Game" the Giants defeat the Chicago Bears for the NFL championship.

1954—Young Vince Lombardi becomes an assistant coach.

1967—The Giants trade for quarterback Fran Tarkenton.

1976—Giants Stadium in East Rutherford, New Jersey, becomes the team's new home facility.

1986—Super Bowl XXI: Giants 39, Broncos 20.

THE BUDDY SYSTEM

The Frankford Yellowjackets were in the middle of the Depression in 1933. It wasn't because they hadn't won any games—the world economy was in a depression, meaning it was in bad shape. People couldn't find jobs anywhere and the Yellowjackets were for sale.

Energetic Bert Bell and partner Lud Wray scraped up the money to buy the team and moved it to Philadelphia. There, Bell renamed the Yellowjackets the Philadelphia Eagles. The Eagle was the symbol of President Franklin D. Roosevelt's efforts to help the United States recover from the Depression.

After 14 years in Philadelphia, the Eagles were runners-up to the Chicago Cardinals in the 1947 NFL championship game. The next they

New York Giants head coach Bill Parcells during a sideline conference with quarterback Phil Simms.

Head coach
Buddy Ryan of the Philadelphia Eagles

It wasn't until Dick Vermeil became the fifth Eagles coach in nine years when he joined the team in 1976 that the team became a force in the NFC Eastern Division. Behind the solid play of quarterback Ron Jaworski, running back Wilbert Montgomery and wide receiver Harold Carmichael, Vermeil led the Eagles to the playoffs in four straight years from 1978 to 1981. In 1981 they reached Super Bowl XV, their first title game in 21 years, but lost to the Oakland Raiders, 27–10.

Coach Buddy Ryan took over the Eagles in 1986 after spending eight seasons as defensive coordinator for the Chicago Bears. Ryan's swaggering attitude got results from the team which has contended for the title nearly every year since then. Ryan is a motivator. He has been a coach with three Super Bowl teams; the 1968 Jets, 1976 Vikings and 1985 Bears.

Winning in Philadelphia is truly a team effort. The Eagles are blessed with several stars but they win games because nobody is selfish. Defensive end Reggie White, the "Minister of Defense," is the best sack artist in the NFL. Quarterback Randall Cunningham is a slick performer. Cunningham's balance, speed and passing make the Eagles' offense something to watch. Add Ryan's leadership and the Eagles are bound for greater heights.

beat the Cardinals, 7–0, to win it, then made it two titles in a row in 1949.

A heavy snow was falling on the day of the 1948 championship. When the Eagles star fullback Steve Van Buren woke up and looked out of his window, he thought the game would surely be postponed and went back to bed. A little later, Van Buren got a frantic call from coach Earle "Greasy" Neale. The game was on! Van Buren raced to the stadium and barely got there in time to get in on the action. He ended up scoring the game's only touchdown.

In the next 33 years the Eagles had little to cheer about though they defeated Green Bay for the 1960 NFL championship. Financial difficulties and frequent coaching changes helped keep the Eagles at the bottom of the league most of the time. But in the early 1960s young quarterback Sonny Jurgensen proved himself one of the best passers in the game and kept some fans interested in the Eagles. (Jurgensen moved to the Washington Redskins in 1964 for Norm Snead.)

TIME LINE

1933—Bert Bell and Lud Wray buy the Frankford Yellowjackets, move them to Philadelphia and rename them the Eagles.

1948—The Eagles win their first NFL championship in a driving snowstorm.

1949—Eagles beat the Los Angeles Rams for the NFL title.

1959—Bert Bell, now the NFL commissioner, dies suddenly of a heart attack watching the Eagles play.

1960—Eagles defeat Green Bay for the NFL title.

1976—Dick Vermeil is named head coach.

1981—Super Bowl XV: Raiders 27, Eagles 10.

1986—Buddy Ryan is named head coach.

TROUBLE IN THE DESERT

In 1988 the Cardinals pulled out of St. Louis and headed for Phoenix, Arizona. The Cardinals owner, Bill Bidwill, was hoping to find some financial relief under the desert sun. In St. Louis his team was so bad that the fans wouldn't pay to see their games. Bidwill hoped things would change in Phoenix.

Wrong. The bad players who were bad in St. Louis were just as bad in Phoenix. Without good players head coach Gene Stallings couldn't win. So he was fired during the middle of the 1989 season even though it wasn't his fault.

Things weren't always bad for the Cardinals. The team began almost a century ago in Chicago. Even though they haven't won many titles, the Cardinals have been trying longer than just about any other team. Chris O'Brien formed the team on Chicago's South Side in 1899 and named them after the color of the faded red jerseys he bought from the University of Chicago. Twice the team was dissolved and reformed.

Ernie Nevers, a legend of football's early days, came out of retirement in 1929 to play for and coach the Cardinals. He scored a record 40 points with six touchdowns and two field goals against the Chicago Bears. In 1960 the NFL moved the team from Chicago to St. Louis to keep the rival AFL from starting a team there.

Since 1920 the Phoenix franchise has had 31 head coaches. The last time the Cardinals won an NFL championship, Harry Truman was president of the United States. The year was 1947, 22 seasons after they won their only other title. In 1974 the Cardinals made their first playoff appearance in 27 years. They managed to win their division in 1975 and 1982. But since 1982 they haven't come close.

The outlook isn't good either. Quarterback Neil Lomax, a star for the Cardinals for several years, probably will never play again because of an injured left hip. Running back Stump Mitchell is nearing the end of a brilliant career. The Cardinals are looking forward to success in the future but they'll need a lot of help before the team becomes a contender again.

TIME LINE

1899—Chris O'Brien forms a neighborhood football team on Chicago's South Side.

1921—Famous player John "Paddy" Driscoll becomes player-coach.

1922—Formerly the Racine Cardinals because they play near Chicago's Racine Avenue, the team becomes officially the Chicago Cardinals.

1932—Ernie Nevers retires.

1947—The Cardinals defeat the Philadelphia Eagles to win the NFL championship.

1948—In a heavy snow, the Eagles beat the Cardinals in an NFL championship rematch.

1960—The Cardinals move to St. Louis.

1974—The Cardinals make the playoffs for the first time since 1947.

1975—St. Louis repeats as NFC East champion.

1982—The Cardinals win their division.

1986—Gene Stallings is hired.

1988—The Cardinals move to Phoenix, Arizona.

Quarterback Neil Lomax of the Phoenix Cardinals

125

Quarterback Doug Williams of the Washington Redskins

REDSKINS ON A RAMPAGE

The San Francisco 49ers won the contest for "Team of the Eighties," but the Washington Redskins were the obvious choice for runner-up. Under Coach Joe Gibbs, the Redskins have played in three Super Bowls in the 1980s and won two of them.

When the Redskins won Super Bowl XVII over Miami in 1983, quarterback Joe Theismann and bulldozing runner John Riggins powered the team to its first NFL championship in 41 years. Another outstanding quarterback, Doug Williams, threw for 340 yards in Super Bowl XXII as

Washington pounded the Denver Broncos, 42–10. In the second quarter of that game the Redskins scored a record 35 points. If Theismann and his teammates hadn't been on the short end of a 38–9 loss to the Los Angeles Raiders in Super Bowl XIX, the 49ers would have had to share their "Team of the Eighties" title.

Gibbs, who came to Washington in 1981, continued a Redskin tradition begun by George Allen 10 years earlier. Allen assembled a group of veterans who came to be known as the "Over-the-Hill Gang" because they were older players. Though most were considered washed up they went all the way to Super Bowl VII in 1973 before losing to the Miami Dolphins. Ten years later, when Gibbs took guys like Theismann, Williams and Riggins to their first Super Bowl, they were nearly old enough to qualify as "Over-the-Hill Gang, Part Two."

The Washington Redskins were founded in Boston in 1932 by George Preston Marshall and christened the Boston Braves after the city's baseball team. In 1937 they moved to Washington, D.C. Marshall was an inventive owner. He suggested that the league be divided into divisions with a championship game, that a different ball be used to help passers and that the goalposts be moved to the goal line. He also brought Slingin' Sammy Baugh to the Redskins. Baugh generated a lot of interest among fans in Washington.

In memorable performances, the Redskins won the NFL championship in 1937 and 1942. But sandwiched between them was the 1940 NFL title game when the Chicago Bears trounced them in the biggest rout the NFL has ever seen, 73–0.

In 1964 the Redskins took their fans by surprise by trading their starting quarterback, Norm Snead, to the Philadelphia Eagles for veteran quarterback Sonny Jurgensen. Anyone who doubted the wisdom of the swap was soon proven wrong. On November 28, 1965, Jurgensen sparked what was at the time the greatest comeback in Redskin history. After trailing 21–0 to the Dallas Cowboys, Jurgensen passed for more than 400 yards and three touchdowns to lead Washington to 34–31 victory. By 1967 Jurgensen had set new Redskin and NFL passing records for most attempts, completions and yards passing. He retired in 1975 after 18 years in the NFL, second on the all-time Redskin list in passing, with 22,585 yards (behind Joe Theismann's 25,206) and in touchdowns, with 179 to Sammy Baugh's 187.

Vince Lombardi and Earl "Curly" Lambeau, who were both associated with the glory of the Green Bay Packers, ended their careers as Redskins coaches. Lambeau retired after 231 wins in the NFL. Lombardi died in 1970 after becoming head coach, executive vice president and a part owner of the team.

Recently Gibbs has looked to strengthen his team through acquiring veterans once again. He traded for seasoned running backs Gerald Riggs and Ernest Byner. Teaming them with young quarterback Mark Rypien and veteran receiver Art Monk, Gibbs hopes to blend youth and experience to make the Super Bowl once more. Linebacker Wilber Marshall came to Washington from the Chicago Bears. He's helping shore up a defensive unit that includes end Charles Mann and cornerback Darrell Green.

TIME LINE

1932—The Redskins are founded as the Boston Braves by George Preston Marshall.

1937—The Redskins move to Washington, D.C., where they win the NFL championship.

1940—The Chicago Bears bury the Redskins, 73–0, in the NFL title game.

1942—The Redskins beat the Bears for the NFL title.

1953—Earl "Curly" Lambeau retires.

1964—The Redskins sign future star quarterback Sonny Jurgensen, who will become one of the NFL's best passers.

1970—Vince Lombardi dies after becoming head coach, part owner and executive vice-president of the Redskins.

1973—Super Bowl VII: Dolphins 14, Redskins 7.

1981—Joe Gibbs is hired as head coach.

1983—Super Bowl XVII: Redskins 27, Dolphins 17.

1985—Super Bowl XIX: Raiders 38, Redskins 9.

1988—Super Bowl XXII: Redskins 42, Broncos 10.

CHAPTER 12

RECORDS

SUPER BOWL RESULTS

Season	Date	Winner	Loser
XXIV	1-28-90	San Francisco	Denver
XXIII	1-22-89	San Francisco	Cincinnati
XXII	1-31-88	Washington	Denver
XXI	1-25-87	N.Y. Giants	Denver
XX	1-26-86	Chicago	New England
XIX	1-20-85	San Francisco	Miami
XVIII	1-22-84	L.A. Raiders	Washington
XVII	1-30-83	Washington	Miami
XVI	1-24-82	San Francisco	Cincinnati
XV	1-25-81	Oakland	Philadelphia
XIV	1-20-80	Pittsburgh	LA Rams
XIII	1-21-79	Pittsburgh	Dallas
XII	1-15-78	Dallas	Denver
XI	1-9-77	Oakland	Minnesota
X	1-18-76	Pittsburgh	Dallas
IX	1-12-75	Pittsburgh	Minnesota
VIII	1-31-74	Miami	Minnesota
VII	1-14-73	Miami	Washington
VI	1-16-72	Dallas	Miami
V	1-17-71	Baltimore	Dallas
IV	1-11-70	Kansas City	Minnesota
III	1-12-69	N.Y. Jets	Baltimore
II	1-14-68	Green Bay	Oakland
I	1-15-67	Green Bay	Kansas City

Score	Site	Attendance
55–10	New Orleans, LA	72,919
20–16	Miami, FL	75,179
42–10	San Diego, CA	73,302
39–20	Pasadena, CA	101,063
46–10	New Orleans, LA	73,818
38–16	Stanford, CA	84,059
38–9	Tampa, FL	72,920
27–17	Pasadena, CA	103,667
26–21	Pontiac, MI	81,270
27–10	New Orleans, LA	76,135
31–19	Pasadena, CA	103,985
35–31	Miami, FL	79,484
27–10	New Orleans, LA	75,583
32–14	Pasadena, CA	103,438
21–17	Miami, FL	80,187
16–6	New Orleans, LA	80,997
24–7	Houston, TX	71,882
14–7	Los Angeles, CA	90,182
24–3	New Orleans, LA	81,023
16–3	Miami, FL	79,204
23–7	New Orleans, LA	80,562
16–7	Miami, FL	75,389
33–14	Miami, FL	75,546
35–10	Los Angeles, CA	61,946

XXIV	QB Joe Montana, San Francisco	XII	DT Randy White and DE Harvey Martin, Dallas
XXIII	WR Jerry Rice, San Francisco	XI	WR Fred Biletnikoff, Oakland
XXII	QB Doug Williams, Washington	X	WR Lynn Swann, Pittsburgh
XXI	QB Phil Simms, N.Y. Giants	IX	RB Franco Harris, Pittsburgh
XX	DE Richard Dent, Chicago	VIII	RB Larry Csonka, Miami
XIX	QB Joe Montana, San Francisco	VII	Safety Jake Scott, Miami
XVIII	RB Marcus Allen, L.A. Raiders	VI	QB Roger Staubach, Dallas
XVII	RB John Riggins, Washington	V	LB Chuck Howley, Dallas
XVI	QB Joe Montana, San Francisco	IV	QB Len Dawson, Kansas City
XV	QB Jim Plunkett, Oakland	III	QB Joe Namath, N.Y. Jets
XIV	QB Terry Bradshaw, Pittsburgh	II	QB Bart Starr, Green Bay
XIII	QB Terry Bradshaw, Pittsburgh	I	QB Bart Starr, Green Bay

NFL CHAMPIONS: 1920-1965

1920	Akron Pros	1942	Washington
1921	Chicago Staleys (renamed the Chicago Bears in 1922)	1943	Chicago Bears
		1944	Green Bay
1922	Canton Bulldogs	1945	Cleveland Rams
1923	Canton Bulldogs	1946	Chicago Bears
1924	Cleveland Bulldogs	1947	Chicago Cardinals
1925	Chicago Cardinals	1948	Philadelphia
1926	Frankford, PA	1949	Philadelphia
1927	N.Y. Giants	1950	Cleveland
1928	Providence Steamrollers	1951	L.A. Rams
1929	Green Bay	1952	Detroit
1930	Green Bay	1953	Detroit
1931	Green Bay	1954	Cleveland
1932	Chicago Bears	1955	Cleveland
1933	Chicago Bears	1956	N.Y. Giants
1934	N.Y. Giants	1957	Detroit
1935	Detroit	1958	Baltimore
1936	Green Bay	1959	Baltimore
1937	Washington	1960	Philadelphia
1938	N.Y. Giants	1961	Green Bay
1939	Green Bay	1962	Green Bay
1940	Chicago Bears	1963	Chicago
1941	Chicago Bears	1964	Cleveland
		1965	Green Bay

AFL CHAMPIONS: 1960-1965

1960	Houston	1964	Buffalo
1961	Houston	1965	Buffalo
1962	Dallas		
1963	San Diego		

ALL-TIME LEADERS

NFL HEAD COACHES — WINS

(as of the 1989 season, including playoffs)

George Halas	325	Hank Stram	136
Don Shula	279	Weeb Ewbank	134
Tom Landry	271	Sid Gillman	123
Curly Lambeau	229	George Allen	120
Chuck Noll	183	Don Coryell	114
Paul Brown	170	John Madden	112
Bud Grant	168	Buddy Parker	107
Steve Owen	153	Vince Lombardi	106
Chuck Knox	155	Bill Walsh	102

RUSHING YARDAGE

Name	Years	Attempts	Yards	Average Yards per Attempt	Touchdowns
Walter Payton	13	3,838	16,726	4.4	110
Tony Dorsett	12	2,936	12,739	4.3	77
Jim Brown	9	2,359	12,312	5.2	106
Franco Harris	13	2,949	12,120	4.1	91
John Riggins	14	2,916	11,352	3.9	104
O. J. Simpson	11	2,404	11,236	4.7	61
Eric Dickerson	6	2,136	9,915	4.6	75
Earl Campbell	8	2,187	9,407	4.3	74
Jim Taylor	10	1,941	8,597	4.4	83
Joe Perry	14	1,737	8,378	4.8	53
Otis Anderson	11	1,949	8,294	4.3	55
Larry Csonka	11	1,891	8,081	4.3	64
Mike Pruitt	11	1,844	7,378	4.0	51
Leroy Kelly	10	1,727	7,274	4.2	74
George Rogers	7	1,692	7,176	4.2	54
Marcus Allen	7	1,712	6,982	4.1	61
John Henry Johnson	13	1,571	6,803	4.3	48
Freeman McNeil	8	1,525	6,794	4.5	28
Wilbert Montgomery	9	1,540	6,789	4.4	45
Chuck Muncie	9	1,561	6,702	4.3	71

PASSING YARDAGE

Name	Years	Attempts	Completions	Completion Percentage	Yards
Fran Tarkenton	18	6,467	3,686	57.0	47,003
Dan Fouts	15	5,604	3,297	58.8	43,040
Johnny Unitas	18	5,186	2,830	54.6	40,239
Ken Anderson	16	4,475	2,654	59.3	32,838

Sonny Jurgensen	18	4,262	2,433	57.1	32,224
John Brodie	17	4,491	2,469	55.0	31,548
Roman Gabriel	16	4,498	2,366	52.6	29,444
Len Dawson	19	3,741	2,136	57.1	28,711
Y. A. Tittle	15	3,817	2,118	55.5	28,339
Ken Stabler	15	3,793	2,270	59.8	27,938
Joe Namath	13	3,762	1,886	50.1	27,663
Joe Montana	10	3,673	2,322	63.2	27,533
George Blanda	26	4,007	1,911	47.7	26,920
Bobby Layne	15	3,700	1,814	49.0	26,768
Joe Theismann	12	3,602	2,044	56.7	25,206
Bob Griese	14	3,429	1,926	56.2	25,092
Bart Starr	16	3,149	1,808	57.4	24,718
Dan Marino	6	3,100	1,866	60.2	23,856
Norm Van Brocklin	12	2,895	1,553	53.6	23,611
Roger Staubach	11	2,958	1,685	57.0	22,700

TOUCHDOWN PASSES

Name	Years	Touchdowns	Interceptions
Fran Tarkenton	18	342	266
Johnny Unitas	18	290	253
Sonny Jurgensen	18	255	189
Dan Fouts	15	254	242
Len Dawson	19	239	183
George Blanda	26	236	277
John Brodie	17	214	224
Y. A. Tittle	15	212	221
Roman Gabriel	15	201	149
Ken Anderson	16	197	160
Dan Marino	6	196	103
Bobby Layne	15	196	243
Ken Stabler	15	194	222
Bob Griese	14	192	172
Joe Montana	10	190	99
Sammy Baugh	16	187	203
Norm Van Brocklin	12	173	178
Joe Namath	13	173	220
Earl Morrall	21	161	148
Joe Theismann	12	160	138

PASS RECEIVING (CATCHES)

Name	Years	Catches	Yards	Yards per Catch	Touchdowns
Steve Largent	13	791	12,686	16.0	97
Charlie Joiner	18	750	12,146	16.2	65
Charley Taylor	13	649	9,110	14.0	79

Don Maynard	15	633	11,834	18.7	88
Raymond Berry	13	631	9,275	14.7	68
Ozzie Newsome	11	610	7,416	12.2	44
James Lofton	11	599	11,085	18.5	54
Harold Carmichael	14	590	8,985	15.2	79
Fred Biletnikoff	14	589	8,974	15.2	76
Harold Jackson	16	579	10,372	17.9	76
Art Monk	9	576	7,979	13.9	39
Lionel Taylor	10	567	7,195	12.7	45
Wes Chandler	11	559	8,966	16.0	56
Lance Alworth	11	542	10,266	18.9	85
Kellen Winslow	10	541	6,741	12.5	45
John Stallworth	14	537	8,723	16.2	63
Bobby Mitchell	11	521	7,954	15.3	65
Nat Moore	13	510	7,546	14.8	74
Dwight Clark	9	506	6,750	13.3	48
Stanley Morgan	12	506	9,866	19.5	64

SUPER BOWL COMPOSITE STANDINGS

Team	Wins	Losses	Won-Lost Percentage	Points Scored	Points Given Up
Pittsburgh	4	0	1.000	103	73
San Francisco	4	0	1.000	84	53
Chicago	2	0	1.000	68	24
N.Y. Giants	1	0	1.000	39	20
N.Y. Jets	1	0	1.000	16	7
Oakland/L.A. Raiders	3	1	.750	111	66
Washington	2	2	.500	85	79
Baltimore	1	1	.500	23	29
Kansas City	1	1	.500	33	42
Dallas	2	3	.400	112	85
Miami	2	3	.400	74	103
L.A. Rams	0	1	.000	19	31
New England	0	1	.000	10	46
Philadelphia	0	1	.000	10	27
Cincinnati	0	2	.000	37	46
Denver	0	4	.000	40	108
Minnesota	0	4	.000	34	95

In professional football, coaches and players speak a special language. It is fascinating to listen to—and sometimes almost impossible to understand. The glossary lets you in on the language of the game and defines most of the important words you'll hear when watching or playing football.

—when the quarterback changes the play at the line of scrimmage and tells the players out loud what the new play is
—short for linebacker
—the area behind the line of scrimmage, on both offense and defense
—whenever a team maintains possession of the ball for a long period, they are said to be "controlling the ball"; teams try to control the ball to keep the other team from scoring points
—an all-out rush by the defense
—a long pass to a wide receiver
—when the quarterback fakes a handoff, hides the football next to his leg and runs the other way
—the weak-side linebacker (away from the tight end)
—combination coverage between the weak safety and strong safety
—1. a pass route, same as flag route; 2. the far corner of one end of the field
—a play in which one or more backs moves away from the point of attack
—when a wide receiver hits a linebacker below his waist; this is illegal but common; sometimes called a crackback block
—the protective pocket that offensive linemen form around their quarterback when he is attempting to pass
—when a lineman blocks his opponent below the knees

—when a running back starts one way and then goes sharply in the opposite direction
—a defense with six defensive backs
—when players other than defensive linemen rush the quarterback
—every time a team runs a play, it is called a down
—a running play that begins like a pass, but is followed by a delayed handoff
—a linebacker covering a pass; he *drops* into a zone
—the touchdown area at both ends of the field
—what a defensive player yells when he makes an interception; this alerts his teammates to block
—a defense with five linemen and three linebackers
—a deep pass route that starts straight down the field but then breaks out toward the flag in the corner of the end zone
—the wide receiver who lines up a yard off the ball and is often the motion man
—a defense in which the linemen are farther off the ball than normal; offensive linemen must "go get" the defensive linemen, which *flexes* the line of scrimmage by opening gaps for linebackers.
—running several receivers into the same zone, which leaves one defender to cover them all
—the direction of a play
—a deep pass route straight down the field
—when a defense turns a play back to the inside
—the way a team, offense or defense, lines up
—a defense with four down linemen and three linebackers
—the defensive line and linebackers
—a trick play, like a reverse
—the space between the offensive linemen
—a deep pass route; same as a fly
—a block by an offensive lineman on a linebacker
—the weak-side (or free) safety
—a defense with six or more defensive linemen
—an alignment or movement that tells the defense where the play is going
—the left cornerback
—the middle linebacker

mac l—the middle linebacker blitzes

mad dog—when all three linebackers blitz

man-for-man—pass coverage in which defensive backs are assigned a specific man

mike—nose tackle

misdirection—using plays that appear to go one way but come back in the other direction

neutral zone—the area between the offensive and defensive lines before the snap

nickel—a defense with five defensive backs

nosetackle—a defensive lineman who lines up right over the center

offside—when a player jumps before the ball is snapped

play action—where the quarterback fakes a handoff but then passes

playbook—a notebook, given to each player on a team, which contains diagrams of every play for that team, both offensively and defensively

pocket—the protective shield offensive linemen form around their quarterback when he is attempting to pass

post—a deep pass in which the receiver starts upfield, then breaks toward the goalpost

power—a running formation that uses three backs in the backfield

prevent—a defense designed to stop long passes; usually used late in a game

pro—a four-three defense

quarter—a defense with seven defensive backs

red dog—a blitz by the strong-side and weak-side linebacker

reverse—when a runner starts in one direction, then hands off to another runner coming back the other way

rose—the right cornerback

sam—the strong-side safety

screen—a pass that develops behind the line of scrimmage; the offensive line allows the defense to penetrate, then forms a wall in front of a running back, to whom the quarterback then throws

secondary—the defensive backfield, which consists of two cornerbacks and two safeties

shield—a block by a wide receiver

short yardage—a defensive formation in which as many as eight players line up on the line of scrimmage

shotgun—a formation in which the quarterback lines up seven yards behind the line of scrimmage

slant—a quick-hitting pass route that slants over the middle

spread—a formation with no running backs at all, but all wide receivers or tight ends

strongside—the side of the formation with the tight end

stub—the strong-side linebacker

stunt—a tactic used by defensive linemen; instead of charging straight ahead, they loop around one another

submarine—when a guard or tackle blocks an opponent below the waist, usually at the knees

trey—a formation with three receivers on wide side and only one fullback behind the quarterback

weak-side—the side of the formation without the tight end

zone—pass coverage in which defenders are assigned a specific area but not a specific receiver

ABOUT THE AUTHOR

Eric Sherman is a free-lance journalist who has written on a variety of topics for newspapers and magazines. When he's not writing about sports, he's often interviewing celebrities for such publications as *TV Guide*, *People*, *Premiere*, *US*, *IN Fashion*, *Redbook* and *Ladies' Home Journal*, where he is a contributing editor. He lives in a very, *very* small apartment in New York City with his cat, Felix.

$1995

DUE DATE

000 962   004 162